SOCIAL SKILLS IN THE EARLY YEARS

Supporting Social and Behavioural Learning

Kay Mathieson

Paul Chapman Publishing

First published 2005

Paul Chapman Publishing
A SAGE Publications Company
1 Oliver's Yard
55 City Road
London EC1Y 1SP

SAGE Publications Inc.
2455 Teller Road
Thousand Oaks, California 91320

SAGE Publications India Pvt Ltd
B-42, Panchsheel Enclave
Post Box 4109
New Delhi 110 017

Library of Congress Control Number: 2004095455

A catalogue record for this book is available from the British Library

ISBN 1 4129 0259 2
ISBN 1 4129 0260 6 (pbk)

Typeset by Pantek Arts Ltd, Maidstone, Kent
Printed in Great Britain by The Cromwell Press, Trowbridge, Wilts.

SOCIAL SKILLS IN THE EARLY YEARS

CONTENTS

ACKNOWLEDGEMENTS

The production of this book would not have happened without the support and help of all my colleagues in Croydon. With the children in their care they have taught me so much about my own behaviour, as well as theirs! Strong influences on my thinking recently have been Ferres Laevers and Colwyn Trevarthen; their enthusiasm is inspirational.

On a personal level a particular thank you to those who have supported me through my writing anxieties either by listening endlessly, proofreading or challenging my thinking.

A very big thank you to the children, parents and staff of Tunstall Nursery School for the use of the photographs, which speak a thousand words! Thank you to Penny Nicholls for organizing everything and a special thank you to Jane Cole for suggesting it in the first place, giving me lots of encouragement and actually taking the photographs.

Finally, a very special thank you to Simone, without whom I would never have begun this journey of discovery about behaviour and social learning.

HOW TO USE THIS BOOK

The purpose of this book is to provide information and guidance about providing for children's social and behavioural learning. The book can be used in a variety of ways depending on the situation and previous experience of the reader. It is arranged in six chapters with a related training session at the end of each chapter. The intended audience for the book includes adults working in day nurseries, schools, pre-schools, nursery classes and toddler groups. The terminology used is a deliberate attempt to be inclusive therefore, any adult working with children is referred to as a 'practitioner' and 'setting' is used to include all of these situations. There is no reference to particular age ranges of children because the principles described can be applied universally. The difference will be in the balance of support provided by the adults. This will be guided by the adults, knowledge of the age, stage and abilities of each individual child.

In terms of maximum impact on everyday practice, the ideal would be for the text and training session to be used by a whole-staff group at the same time. But the experience of working through the training sessions in any group will increase confidence and enable individuals to influence the practice positively in their setting. As an individual, working through the book will provide reinforcement of good practice and prompts to reflect on current experience in any setting.

Although the training sessions are provided to facilitate group discussion and learning, they can also be used to prompt and develop personal reflection. The focus throughout the book is to identify and increase the frequency of observable good practice. The ultimate evidence of the understanding of the information contained in the chapters is that it informs the individual day-to-day practice of the practitioner. This cannot help but lead to improved experience for each child. One of the ways in which the experience of the child is looked at, is through parallel experiences for us as adults. This involves taking time to consider how we feel and what influences our reactions to specific situations. If this is done in a reflective and problem-solving way, it can lead to useful insight which can improve our practice. It does not, however, provide factual knowledge about what someone else is thinking or reasons for their actions. We must be prepared to amend our hypothesis in the light of further experience.

Ultimately, the book is a learning tool to be used as flexibly as possible to suit the particular situation. As learning takes place best in relaxed and happy conditions, I hope your experience of the book is also enjoyable!

INTRODUCTION TO TRAINING SESSIONS

There is a training session following each chapter. These can be used in a variety of ways but the intention is that they will guide the process of sharing ideas and finding ways of improving the experience of the children in the setting. This can be achieved through the adults working together as a team with shared values. If the whole-staff team can be involved in each part of the process, then there is greater likelihood of the children receiving more consistent messages, particularly about their social, emotional, behavioural learning.

The purpose of the training sessions is to highlight the key points made in each chapter. It gives an opportunity to revisit the main points and explore further some of the ideas. The trainer should support participants to examine the ways in which the main ideas are having an impact on day-to-day practice and identify ways in which this can be improved.

It is essential that the training sessions are delivered in ways which are in tune with the principles contained in the text. If we are aiming for practitioners to provide an interesting learning environment, which encourages a relaxed and joyful approach to learning, then we must model this in our training sessions.

The role of trainer should mirror the good practice described related to the role of the adult, namely:

- care
- opportunities to build self-esteem
- appropriate learning opportunities
- a rich learning environment
- a consistent supportive relationship
- emotional and physical safety.

The parallels between child and adult learning in the chapters are clear and should be consciously used in the planning of the training sessions. This will include ensuring that:

1. the room is of a suitable size with appropriate furniture, temperature and light
2. refreshments, especially water, are available and appropriate breaks planned
3. the materials and delivery of the session is well planned and prepared

4 participants have information prior to the session to enable them to make any necessary arrangements, understand the purpose of the training and prepare themselves

5 everyone is sincerely welcomed to the session, the tone is deliberately set as one of opportunity for joint problem-solving and reflection

6 all contributions are welcomed and valued, with the trainer actively engaging with quieter participants to ensure their views are included and heard.

In order to support this approach it can be helpful to:

- display the aims of the session
- outline what will be covered during the session
- suggest or develop some group rules to encourage involvement and support respectful responses to contributions
- have a clear expectation of the likely timings for each element of the session and manage this time effectively
- at the end of the session review the aims, the key points which have been discussed and any action which has been agreed
- give positive feedback about involvement in the session and provide opportunity for participants to give their own feedback.

It is important to remember that adults and children need opportunities to get used to new experiences and ways of working. If the participants in the training session are not used to working together, being able to have their say or discussing their work in this depth, they will need time to feel comfortable. This will include being convinced that the trainer really will respect their contributions and that it is okay to disagree with a suggestion. The trainer will need to manage this experience sensitively, maintaining the agreed rules and the conditions for joint problem-solving. The best preparation, for the trainer, is to consider some likely scenarios and to have in mind phrases and responses which you can deliver confidently to manage the discussion. Reflecting on the positive outcomes of each session will enable the trainer to identify strategies which support the group to engage meaningfully in the activities.

The information about each training session contains:

- identified aims for each session
- photocopiable overhead transparencies (OHTs) which can also be used as handouts
- suggestions of activities to accompany each OHT.

It is not necessary to use every activity, but delivery of the session should take into account the variety of learning styles of the participants. Therefore, it is important to include opportunities for learning through:

- hearing
- seeing
- doing.

The most conclusive evidence of our learning is that we are able to apply it to a variety of practical situations. The use of detailed descriptions can be successfully used as a way of clarifying with colleagues what this would look like in reality. This has the dual advantage of reducing the feelings of self-consciousness when the learning is applied to a real situation, because there is already agreement about the value of the approach or strategy. Inevitably, each participant will learn at a different rate and this will be influenced by several factors over which we have no control.

Constant encouragement and positive reflection of new learning being applied will build confidence and nurture the process between the training sessions. This will then provide the conditions for the best possible chance of success for the participants and improved experience for the children.

Working in Educare

In this chapter the following questions will be considered:

1 What are the main pieces of legislation which affect our work?

2 In what ways are improvements to childcare being made?

3 What differences do we make to children's lives?

Our present working lives are influenced by a variety of legislation. Although each has a separate focus they do complement each other. The key themes are that all children are able to access education and care provision. There are minimum Ofsted standards for all provision. Parents' views are crucial to inclusion for all children. Children's views should be recorded whenever possible. There should be early identification of additional needs with early intervention to prevent further or increased difficulty. Additional needs may be short or long term. There is a responsibility on adults to provide for children's needs appropriately. Personal, social and emotional learning is crucial to all other learning. The high quality of the adult–child interaction is essential to effective and meaningful learning.

The private and voluntary and independent sectors are now being included in the push for higher standards, equity of provision and more focused learning opportunities for all children. There may be some debate about the government's motivation for this but our role, as I see it, is to use the help and support offered to improve the experience of each individual child to the best of our ability. The recent legislation provides us with a framework within which we can provide learning opportunities of a consistent type and quality for all of our children. The documents complement each other and give consistent messages about the importance of experiential learning, realistic expectations of individual children and the essential role of the professional practitioner.

The pace of change in recent years in the Early Years education and childcare sector has been hectic and sometimes confusing. Whilst it feels good to be included and high profile in government thinking, sometimes we look back with rose-coloured spectacles to the quieter days when we were left to get on with the job. What is certainly true however, is that the focus of the changes is about improving quality of provision and equity of opportunity for all children. I feel sure that no one working with children would argue with this as an aim. In our day-to-day work it can be difficult to see how the implementation of some of the legislation positively changes what we do. It is important to remember when this clouds our thinking that the variation in quality of provision, even within a small geographical area, can be enormous. In effect, this means that a child's opportunities are still being left to chance to a large extent. Parents wishing to find good quality childcare provision may have their choices limited by distance, cost, lack of knowledge and by confusion over the range of possibilities. Choosing a good quality childcare or education provision for your child is dependent on your interpretation of what you see and the extent of the information available to you.

It is our responsibility as practitioners to give parents information about our setting which clearly identifies the principles and strengths of our provision, which will then help them to make an informed choice. To ensure that we are giving our children the best possible chance of success we must keep up to date with the changes and new ideas which are a part of the world in which we work. It is also useful now and again to check out why we, as individuals, are working with young children. If we are there to support the children as individuals, working with colleagues to give each child the best possible chance of success in all that they do, then we will get back a sense of making a positive difference to the lives of children and families. There is nothing more demoralizing than turning up to work to watch the clock and feel that everything is getting in the way of you having a 'quiet' day!

The most important aspect of our work is the quality of our interaction and relationship with each individual child, and developing our role of learning companion in their problem- solving.

Specific Legislation

Pieces of legislation now have a significant impact on our context for working. For example,

- Birth to Three Matters framework
- Foundation Stage Curriculum
- Ofsted inspections

- Disability Discrimination Act 1995
- Special Educational Needs Code of Practice (2001)
- Every Child Matters (Green Paper)
- Removing Barriers to Achievement.

I do not propose to cover these in any great detail as further information and the actual documents can be accessed on the Internet, at libraries and in your own setting. However, it is important to identify the level of priority and suggested approaches which are contained in each of these important documents.

The Foundation Stage Curriculum details the experiences and opportunities which should be provided for children in six areas of learning. The introductory sections of the document clearly set the tone of the curriculum, highlighting the need for working to the child's strengths and individual needs, working in partnership with parents and using observation evidence to support any judgements about children's progress.

From the perspective of this book it is significant that the area of personal, social and emotional learning is highlighted by appearing first in order of subject areas and is described as critical to the other areas of learning.

There is clear backing for the belief that personal and social development is the cornerstone of an individual's capacity to make their way in society and to have that sense of emotional well-being. But, the reality is, that as an area of the curriculum, personal and social learning, is probably the most difficult to implement. It is the area which challenges adults most, partly because we are human beings too. The things which we identify as difficult for children are also potentially difficult for us. We must try to remember that the society in which children are growing up today is very different from the one we experienced as children. This means that we cannot know how they feel. We can guess, hypothesize and predict but we do not know. Not only has society moved on but so, too, has the knowledge which is available to us to inform our practice. The knowledge and facts which were once on the university syllabus are now in the secondary or even the primary curriculum. We can accept this as true for science and mathematics but we are less likely to think in this way about understanding how people relate to each other and become socially literate. It is essential that we access and use research findings and guidance such as the Foundation Stage Curriculum to inform our thinking, our everyday practice and to support children's learning.

The key points from Every Child Matters are that:

- information regarding concerns about children should be shared between relevant services
- that a sense of accountability should be encouraged in all adults working with children
- effective training should be available and taken up to improve management and leadership of staff.

Themes which were raised included the fact that help often comes too little, too late and that early identification and planned action will give children a better chance to overcome difficulties and make the best of opportunities available to them. It is also important that Child Protection should not be seen as a separate issue but should inform good practice in our setting. The focus should be on improving things for all children and through establishing professional, respectful relationships with children so that we will be more able to identify difficulties earlier. Action can then have a greater focus on preventing difficulties and mobilizing support from appropriate agencies.

In order to make this happen the document identifies four areas for action:

1 supporting parents and carers
2 early intervention and effective protection
3 accountability and integration of services, locally, regionally and nationally
4 workforce reform.

The most noticeable change in our work in childcare is the change in the inspection process. This is now carried out by the Office for Standards in Education (Ofsted) and covers not only the 'care' aspect of our provision but also the educational opportunities provided for children.

The Ofsted National Standards set out minimum requirements for our provision and form the basis of the inspection process. Within this document is included the need to have key members of staff with responsibility for particular areas such as:

- Special Educational Needs (SEN)
- Behaviour
- Child Protection.

It is important that having these individual responsibilities does not separate the support for the individual child, and that there are planned opportunities for staff to share information and concerns, and for these to be co-ordinated and acted upon for the benefit of the child.

Whilst the Foundation Stage Curriculum is ideal for providing appropriate learning opportunities for the 3–5 age range it obviously does not cater for the 0–3s. The Birth to Three Matters framework is a very effective and supportive pack of information. It clearly places the child at the centre of the learning process and emphasizes the need for supportive caring relationships between the individual child and the adults in the setting. The pack is arranged into four aspects which focus on the competencies of the child. These are identified as the:

- Strong child
- Skilful communicator
- Competent learner
- Healthy child.

Again, there is clear emphasis on the need for children to be supported in developing a sense of well-being and secure relationships with others.

Opportunity to reflect

In what ways have these documents impacted on your everyday practice?

Early Education and Childcare

The implementation of the recent legislation moves our thinking and practice from one of purely care to a combination of education and care. This is now sometimes referred to as educare. However, the reality is that it is virtually impossible to separate the care and education elements of a child's day, no matter which provision they attend. In establishing an early years provision the initial thinking needs to clarify, for all adults involved, the purpose of the provision. This is the point at which the guiding principles and values are formed which will establish the principles of care and education the children will experience. The ideal is to bring together best practice in both care and education. Initially, this seems like a daunting prospect but by using the Ofsted National Standards and the Foundation Stage Curriculum to inform discussion and training, practitioners can clarify what the result of this blend will look like in their setting on a day-to-day basis.

Many children will spend ten hours per day, five days per week in a childcare setting, their experiences will have a significant impact on their future lives.

The children in our care will learn about making relationships and social behaviour every minute they are with us; there is nothing we can do to prevent this. However, the more conscious decisions we make about the way we behave and respond, the more effective and positive this learning is likely to be. In the longer term this should help to make our experience of our day-to-day work more pleasant and effective. The key to achieving this is not easy and involves developing a professional persona which can help us to be realistic about the interpretation of what we see happening. For example, a child who in a temper says 'I hate you' does not have an adult understanding of the implications or meaning of this phrase but is communicating that they are not happy with your decision at this moment in time.

Our role is to help the child deal with their emotions and be able to find a way to maintain the relationship with you even though you are not in agreement at this time. The role you play is not that of parent but of a professional learning guide, identifying the achievements and following the child's interests to identify the appropriate next steps for their learning. If this is done from the perspective of an in-depth knowledge of the individual child and child development, then our expectations will be realistic and our assessment of achievements secure. The keyworker system recommended in each of the discussed documents is an ideal basis for this knowledge and in planning. It adds to the role an element of advocacy for the child, being the one to highlight the child's perspective, interests and strengths in discussion with colleagues and planning.

One of the joys of working with children is getting to know each child and their individual personalities, likes, dislikes, fears, anxieties, strengths and confidences. This is true of any child coming to our setting. We begin finding out about them from the first time we speak to their parent or carer. Sometimes, if that initial discussion contains information about a child's additional or special educational need it can cause anxiety in the adults which leads them to think they are unable to welcome the child into the setting. Regardless of the form or extent of the need, the child is first and foremost a child to get to know, to encourage and with whom to share celebration of successes.

The idea of a fully inclusive Early Years setting is an aim we would all want to work towards. However, putting the theory into practice is not always easy and sometimes needs some considerable changes in our thinking as well as practical adjustments. If we are able to establish principles in our practice, about focusing on what a child can do, as a baseline for our planning and are able to communicate this clearly to parents, then we have a means of being proactive in developing our inclusive practice. Using the phrasing from the Disability Discrimination Act about identifying barriers to participation and learning, we are reminded that the problem is not with the child but with the form in which learning opportunities are offered and the physical environment. Feedback from practitioners confirms that if we focus on improving opportunities for children with additional needs we will have a positive impact on the experience of all children.

Working with children of any age is a challenging and often tiring career. To maintain our interest and enthusiasm it is important to find ways of sharing ideas with colleagues, extending our knowledge and experience, and keeping our qualifications and training up to date. There is never a time when we could say that we know everything about children. Every day the children themselves will teach us something new, if we let them. Also research is uncovering more and more information about how human beings learn and the most effective ways of supporting this learning. If we do nothing to enhance our own learning and development, we are not able to give our children the best possible opportunities for their learning. It is common to see newspaper and television reports which tell us that the behaviour of children is rapidly deteriorating in our schools and communities and involves younger and younger age groups. The children we work with each day are experiencing ways of living which are very different to our own early lives. The speed of change has accelerated and it is almost impossible for organizations and our thinking to keep up. We cannot predict which skills and knowledge our children will need as adults but we can be certain that they will need to be able to sustain relationships with others and have sufficient confidence and self-belief to be able to take on the challenges life presents. The foundation for this learning happens very early in our lives and is affected by all our subsequent experiences. Using the skills we have, we can provide a rich learning environment which allows children to find out about their strengths and weaknesses, to make mistakes, to reflect on their own progress and to gain the confidence to approach new challenges.

TRAINING SESSION 1

The 'Introduction to training sessions' should be considered before delivery of each training session.
This training session relates to the text contained in Chapter 1.

Key Points

1 Main pieces of legislation/guidance.

2 Themes from legislation/guidance.

3 The role of the adult.

4 Inclusion.

5 Opportunities for our own learning.

Notes

Each OHT gives key points about the legislation/guidance taking each piece in turn group discussion can then be focused on how this can have an impact on day-to-day practice in a particular setting.

The aims of this training session are to:

- understand the key points in the documents
- consider the impact of the key points on day-to-day practice
- identify present practice which supports inclusive working
- identify ways in which present practice could be improved.

Activities can be selected from the following suggestions and developed to suit your particular situation. The more detail identified through each of the activities, the more use it will be for practitioners to identify with and be able to put into practice. Guiding the discussion towards producing a clear description of what it would look like in reality can be very helpful.

OHTs 1 and 2

- Introduce names of recent legislation and revise key points. Support participants to share their existing knowledge and understanding of some of the documents named.
- In groups arrange the common themes of the legislation in order of priority and justify the order to the group.
- Formulate descriptions of observable behaviours which would be seen as evidence that the legislation/guidance had been implemented in your setting. For example, practitioners use observation notes to directly inform the planning of activities, which have clear learning outcomes for each child. When considering the Disability Discrimination Act it is important to emphasize that it does not just refer to physical access, but also access in terms of involvement. For example, identifying ways in which a child with challenging behaviour can be included in an outing to the local park or a child with language difficulties can be included in a game.

▶

1 CONTINUED

OHT 3

- Make a list of some activities which practitioners are involved in on a day-to-day basis which fit with each of these common themes. For example, children are encouraged to say what activities they have enjoyed and suggest new activities which are then included in planning.

OHT 4

- Whilst the current legislation and guidance informs our practice as individuals, we have most influence on the actual interactions between ourselves and the children. Opportunities to reflect on the quality of these interactions is rare but essential for identifying ways of improving the child's experience and learning.
- Identify in the group what a 'quality' interaction would look like – how would you describe it in detail? Prompt the discussion to include description of facial expression, body language, tone of voice, words used, ability to be in tune with the child's emotions, response of child.

OHT 5

- Having considered the list, agree with the group what would be involved in 'reflecting.' What question prompts might help to structure your reflective thinking? For example, 'What did I say, how did I say it?'
- Share new learning which has taken place recently for each individual from their day-to-day working. Each item of new learning should be explored to gain as much detail as possible and to suggest possible ways to extend the learning.
- Individually, identify a focus of new learning to explore over the next three weeks. List possible sources for information and exploration. Share your list of sources with the group.

OHT 1
Session 1

Recent legislation and guidance relating to educare

Birth to Three Matters framework

- Babies have an enormous capacity to learn
- Adults can play an essential role in providing appropriate experiences to guide learning
- Young children need to be able to develop relationships with key familiar adults
- Although there are recognizable stages in learning, each child develops as an individual and at their own pace

Foundation Stage Curriculum

- Common approach to learning for children from 3 to 5
- Arranged in six areas of learning
- Personal, social and emotional learning is critical to all other areas
- Stepping stones for each area to support planning

Ofsted Standards

- Minimum requirements for settings
- Combined inspections to cover education and care aspects of provision

Disability Discrimination Act

- Encouraging inclusive approaches for all
- Requirement to make reasonable adjustments to enable access to setting and involvement in activities

OHT 2
Session 1

Recent legislation and guidance relating to Educare

SEN Code of Practice

- Parents and children's involvement in the process essential
- Graduated response to children's needs
- Early Years Action, Early Years Action Plus
- Encourages early identification and intervention
- Professionals from different agencies share information and work together with parents

Every Child Matters

- Families should be able to tell their story to one lead person who will co-ordinate support
- Support services should share information for the benefit of the child and family
- Focus should be on finding ways to meet children's needs

Removing Barriers to Achievement

- Early identification and intervention
- Preventative programmes of support
- Training for adults working with children
- All sectors (private, voluntary, maintained and independent) working together
- Professionals from different agencies must share information and work together

OHT 3
Session 1

Common themes in the legislation and guidance

- All children able to access educare provision
- Minimum Ofsted standards for all provision
- Parents' views crucial to inclusion for all children
- Children's views to be recorded whenever possible
- Early identification of additional needs
- Additional needs may be short or long term
- Responsibility on adults to provide appropriately for children's needs
- Early intervention to reduce further difficulty or identify specific focus of future support
- Personal, social and emotional learning crucial to all other learning
- Quality of the adult–child interaction is essential

OHT 4
Session 1

High-quality adult–child interactions are essential

Adult role is to provide:

- care
- opportunities to build self-esteem
- appropriate learning opportunities
- a rich learning environment
- a consistent supportive relationship
- emotional and physical safety
- a positive and supportive communication link with parents

OHT 5
Session 1

Opportunities for adult learning

- Observing and reflecting on what helps children learn
- Challenging our assumptions about individuals
- Finding out more about how we communicate with each other
- Finding out more about child development
- Getting to know what individual children really like about the setting
- Sharing our understanding of individual children with parents
- Listening to parents' understanding of their children
- Reflecting with a colleague about ways of building individual children's self-esteem
- Attending specific training courses
- Taking further qualifications

CHAPTER 2

Helping Young Children Learn

In this chapter the following questions will be considered:

1 What can we do to help learning to take place?

2 How do we decide if our expectations of children are realistic?

3 How can we encourage and support adult learning?

In reality our expectations of children are very high, especially socially. Children of today have a very different social life than previous generations. What we do as adults will make a difference to the children's experience and their learning. Being clear about, and agreeing with colleagues, what messages we want to give about the values and principles guiding our practice will make it easier to make these a reality. Understanding the learning process can help us to apply the principles to social, emotional and behavioural learning. By breaking down the steps needed to achieve a task we can be more realistic about our expectations of children's achievements. As adults we need to be developing our own learning about the children we work with and the way in which they learn.

One area of agreement when thinking about Early Years settings is that learning takes place extensively. It would be easy to be complacent and not to think any further about this learning. After all we want children to learn, and they do, so what more do we need to consider? However, to think about what children learn and how they learn starts to open out the discussion. My suggestion would be that children and adults are learning every minute of every day. The consequence of this is that some of the things learned are helpful, others are not so helpful. Equally, the way in which the learning takes place can be either a positive or negative experience. As usual, what initially seems to be a simple statement becomes more complex the longer you think about it.

Making our settings positive and rich learning environments has a great deal more to do with attitudes and values than with the bricks and mortar. To provide such an environment there needs to be some conscious decisions made by the adults involved. A useful place to start is to identify the five key messages which they would like to communicate about the setting. This might include statements such as:

- Everyone will be welcomed to the setting.
- Relationships will be based on respect and valuing each other.
- Learning opportunities will be planned based on what children can do.
- Learning is fun.
- Physical and emotional safety are given the highest priority.

The hard bit is how to make these ideals become a reality and to involve the whole community of the setting in the process. Having established the five statements, the discussion needs to go a step further and describe what would be seen if each of the statements were achieved. For example, how will each adult and child be welcomed to the setting. This includes staff, parents, children and visitors. The more people who can be involved in this process the more effective it is likely to be. By asking for feedback from everyone about how they would like to be welcomed and if they feel welcomed, you will be able to develop and improve your practice. This process can be applied to each of the statements in turn and the result will be a set of descriptions of how you want things to be. This clear shared understanding of what everyone wants the setting to be like, helps to also communicate the expectations of behaviour and response to everyone.

The first time this discussion takes place all staff will be involved. But it cannot be a one-off event, otherwise, once the novelty has worn off, the changes will not be maintained. To ensure that the key messages become embedded in day-to-day practice, they need to be introduced and sustained at several levels. This will include:

- management commitment
- introduction and discussion at staff meetings
- follow-up support to implement changes
- positive displays around the setting to share the decisions
- proactive development of a culture of adults supporting each other

- management support on progress of implemented changes
- regular review of progress and refocus of efforts
- key messages and record of discussion used in induction programme for new staff
- inclusion of key messages as item in appraisal discussion
- feedback to and from parents about positive impact of approach
- regular feedback to staff about the impact of their positive responses
- opportunities to share worries in joint problem-solving discussions between colleagues
- management monitoring of observable behaviour which fits with key messages.

Essential to making these key messages part of our everyday practice is the need to have realistic expectations both of the children and ourselves.

Expectations of Children and Ourselves

In order to make informed professional decisions about ways of meeting the needs of the children in our care, we have to have a sound knowledge of child development. It is obvious that we would not expect a child to be able to have the same level of understanding or skill as an adult. But, it is not so clear how different the level of understanding could be between two children of similar age. We make assumptions and judgements about children's understanding every minute of our working day, and it is useful to think about what we can do to ensure that these judgements are fair and supportive to children's learning.

First, basic knowledge of child development is essential. Most childcare qualifications include child development, but it is important to review this knowledge regularly. The Birth to Three materials provide strong support for increasing knowledge of child development to guide us to have realistic ideas about what children of different ages are likely to be able to achieve. The literature review element of the materials provides a comprehensive and stimulating collection of information. The developmental descriptors,

- Heads-up lookers and communicators
- Sitters standers and explorers
- Movers, shakers and players
- Walkers, talkers and pretenders,

leads the reader to a positive view of a child's competencies. These titles support an approach based on the individual child's developmental stage rather than overemphasizing their age. There is also clear recognition that children will be developing a range of skills and abilities from the four aspects at the same time. There is obvious continuity between Birth to Three Matters framework and the Foundation Stage Curriculum which, hopefully, will soon be extended to support Key Stage 1 children. With the support of these materials we can then use our knowledge of the individual child to ensure that our expectations are realistic. Sharing our thinking with colleagues will help to keep our judgements relevant to the children in our setting at any one time.

This is particularly true of behaviour and language learning. It is much easier to make judgements about appropriate learning of skills such as moving around and joining construction materials than about behaviour and language skills. As far as language is concerned it can be very difficult to assess the child's level of understanding. Children spend a long time playing with language and trying out phrases and words which they collect from each other and the adults around them. Unfortunately, when we learn a word we do not always learn the meaning too. Having learnt the meaning this does not guarantee that we fully comprehend the effect or power of the words we are using. As adults, we need to be careful not to assume that because a child uses a particular phrase that they fully understand its meaning or implication. Children can often copy the intonation and context before they understand the meaning of specific language. This is particularly true of emotional outbursts, 'I hate you' from a three year old is more likely to mean 'I really do want to play with that toy now' rather than a strong personal dislike of you as a person. Looking for the meaning behind the phrase is essential if we are going to help children develop and use their vocabulary appropriately. If you have limited words to choose from you will inevitably select the nearest 'best fit' to how you feel. Equally, as adults our understanding of a particular phrase may be different to a colleague's.

Opportunity to reflect

Try to identify common phrases which are used in the setting by different adults particularly about behaviour. In what ways can they be amended to give a clearer and more positive message to children?

Use of language evolves over time. Meanings and associations change and have different levels of importance in different cultures. An obvious example is using the word 'naughty' which used to be commonly used in response to inappropriate behaviour. As our understanding and knowledge of children's learning has developed, we have come to realise that telling a child they are naughty labels them as something we disapprove of and provides them with no clue as to how this could be changed. As they continue to hear the label attached to them by different adults they develop the belief that the behaviour and the label belongs to them. This can then lead them to live up to the label. As a basic principle we are now much more aware that we need to separate the child from the behaviour. So, clearly we must identify that we continue to like and care about the child but are not happy about the particular behaviour. Helping children to see themselves as being able to succeed in developing appropriate behavioural skills is essential to this becoming a reality. This belief will be supported through positive approaches from the adults but can also be encouraged through the use of photographs which focus on previous successes. The role that self-esteem plays in our developing understanding about behaviour cannot be underestimated. If we believe that we are not as good as others, are not able to succeed at anything, this will become a barrier to our learning and especially our social connections.

Sharing our understanding and knowledge about individual children with colleagues can help to protect and enhance the child's self-esteem. We must encourage each other to have a positive view of the child's ability to learn, given the right support.

Equally, our expectations of ourselves and the other adults in the setting must be based in the real world or we quickly become dispirited about the pace of progress in children's learning. Attributing 'blame' to a colleague when a child behaves inappropriately is unlikely to develop effective strategies which will support the child's learning.

The Learning Process – How Does It Happen?

When we are learning something new there are various stages we go through usually including the following:

- Watching others
- Trying ourselves
- Breaking down some of the skills
- Practising skills separately
- Fitting the separate skills together
- Applying the skills to a variety of situations
- Improving our skill level through rehearsal and repetition.

These stages do not necessarily take place in this order or one at a time, and our individual learning style will determine which stage has most impact on us.

There are basic elements which ensure a reasonable chance that learning will take place. If we are able to clearly identify and use these to guide our practice then we can apply them to any child's learning. One of the key issues is self-esteem. Research suggests that we all learn best when in a relaxed, happy but attentive mood. This is best achieved if the learning is presented in a way which increases our self-esteem. This means we need to link any new learning to some previous successful learning. This helps to make the approach to the activity more relaxed and encourages an openness to learning. Most of us approach a new or unfamiliar activity with some level of anxiety. If we think we are going to fail or find it very difficult, our anxiety obviously increases. Other barriers to learning related to self-esteem include having some idea of the response we are likely to get from those around us, especially if they are important to us.

- The way we see ourselves in relation to those around us will have a major impact on the way in which we approach a task and the confidence we have in our own success.
- The way we see ourselves develops through a combination of responses we get from other people and our perception of our relative success or failure in things we do.
- Adults can use this knowledge to present appropriate activities in an interesting and inviting way, and to help children meet the manageable challenges of the activities.

What is often overlooked is that these principles apply to both adult and child learning.

Research continues to discover the extensive capacity children have for learning. The work of Professor Colwyn Trevarthen (Trevarthen, 1993) about babies' communication is evidence of how early and how rapidly children are able to learn. Needless to say, not everyone learns at the same rate, in the same way or will learn exactly the same thing from the same experience. This makes our day seem like a cocktail of possibilities and unknowns. However, using our basic practice of observation and assessment to identify appropriate next steps and learning experiences, we can break down the process into manageable steps.

Small Steps

A long journey begins with one small step. No matter how hard the task or new learning, it is possible to break it down into small steps which can then make the process manageable. This is true of both adult and child learning. If this approach is combined with realistic expectations of those involved, then we have the makings of a dynamic and effective learning opportunity. By exploring with colleagues the various elements which make up a child successfully completing an activity, we can be more realistic in our expectations of their progress. This is not to say that we will teach the child each step in isolation, but it can help us to realize just how much we are asking of children in a single activity. It can also contribute to our problem-solving process by enabling us to identify the parts of the process which are easily managed by the child. As a consequence it will also then give us some information about difficulties which are occurring. The action taken by the adults, informed by these observations will involve finding a variety of ways of helping the child to develop and explore the necessary skills.

For example, in order to have their snack a child needs to:

1. leave previous the activity
2. move to the snack table
3. find a space
4. find a chair
5. sit on the chair
6. ask for a drink
7. hold a cup
8. convey thanks
9. drink
10. put the cup down
11. stand up
12. move away from the table,

as well as manage relationships with all the children and adults around.

Having broken the activity down we can then identify the 'can do' statements for the particular child or group. This provides the opportunity to give specific praise for the achievements and focus our teaching support on the next small step of learning which is needed. For example, through reviewing the breakdown of the task we may be able to identify that the child can achieve the first five steps but that difficulties regularly occur at the point when the child is expected to ask for the drink. This realization can lead to an exploration of the possible reasons for this being a difficult part of the process. There are many possibilities and these may relate to language skills, understanding, shyness, anxiety, adult communication of what the child needs to do, unrealistic expectations of the child 'performing', response of other children or response of adult. The list is virtually endless, but in identifying exactly where in the process the difficulty occurs, practitioners can work together to review observations to inform problem-solving ways of helping the child to achieve this next step. There needs to be a balance between looking at the learning which needs to take place for the child, and what the adult actions will be in order to make this learning not only possible, but inevitable. This ensures the view that the adult role is to be an active participant in the child's learning, rather than setting targets which are mountains which have to be climbed.

Inclusion

Putting together the idea of identifying the barriers to participation and learning, with this small-step approach, can give us a process which can be applied to any situation. Using the opportunity to share the problem-solving with parents and colleagues in the setting is essential to increase the chances of finding a workable solution. No one person can think of every possible aspect of a problem or solution, but in discussion with others the benefit of joint thinking is a shorter journey to a good strategy. The same joint thinking needs to be applied when reviewing strategies, especially if we did not get the response we were expecting. For this collaboration between children, parents and practitioners to become a reality, the communication links need to be firmly established from day one and steadily built on each day. This communication is our provision's best publicity; it should communicate the essence of the principles which inform practice within the setting on a day-to-day basis. This is not easy to deliver, particularly as the contact between practitioners and parents takes place at the worst times of day: First, when parents are rushing to work after a fraught morning; secondly, at the end of a long hard day (for everyone). These are often quite daunting interactions for practitioners, particularly new staff, but it is also difficult for parents. Parents may be struggling with feelings of guilt about leaving the child, concern about what may happen to them during the day and fear of being judged by staff because of their abilities or behaviour. Quite a cocktail of emotion and stress can develop, so conscious thought needs to be given to how this can be successfully managed.

This conscious thought should be directed to applying our knowledge of communication and learning to include parents and children in the learning process. For example, we have identified that working in partnership with parents enhances the practitioners' effectiveness in supporting children's learning. If we explore this further it is possible to identify some of the key issues.

It is likely that parents have little or no experience of similar Early Years provision themselves. Providing information such as:

- principles and values
- the outline of the day
- opportunities to talk with staff
- methods of communication
- approaches to behaviour
- use of the keyworker system.

Anything we can do which includes parents in the experience of their child's educare will help to reduce anxiety and build confidence in the provision.

1. Parents are often trying to balance challenging tensions of work and home, which may result in feelings of guilt or inadequacy.
2. Practitioners can be proactive in taking the first step in the relationship and welcoming parents to share in the life of the setting. This need not involve them being physically present in the setting but being included in the sharing of news and information about what is going on within the setting. The more practitioners are able to communicate the essence of what life in the setting is like, the more parents are likely to be supportive and to work in partnership.
3. If the positive relationship described above is achieved, practitioners are more likely to understand some of the issues and cultural influences and how these may affect the child's learning.
4. Making inclusive practice a reality is based on positive attitude, clear communication and a secure framework for positive relationships.
5. If these positive relationships are established from the first contact with the setting then, should any specific issues need to be discussed, these can be done within the context of this relationship.
6. Viewing partnership working with parents as an investment for your organization can open up your thinking and ensure that some staff time is made available for the conscious development of structures and practices which provide a framework for these relationships to be established and maintained.

Inevitably, as individuals we develop quicker and easier relationships with some people than others. In setting up processes which encourage positive relationships with parents it is important to clarify what we would expect this to look like. We should not be trying to be a best friend or a distant professional but somewhere in between. Working with colleagues to collect descriptive statements about how the relationship should look can help to clarify our shared understanding of what we are trying to achieve. For example:

- All adults in the setting will smile and greet parents they encounter in the setting.
- All adults in the setting will ask if they can help parents they encounter in the setting.
- Keyworkers will approach parents and share news of the day including the child in conversation.
- Keyworkers will provide parents with positive news of the child's achievements and enjoyment in the day.

- keyworkers will share concerns at the earliest opportunity and in the context of what they have observed, and with suggestions about how they will begin to help the child overcome any difficulties.
- managers will talk to parents with keyworkers on a regular basis to share both achievements and concerns.

Clarifying what is expected in discussion will also raise issues about ways of developing staff expertise in improving their skills in communicating with parents. Managers and senior staff are inevitably role models for the rest of the staff in terms of their relationships with parents, but also in interactions with children. It is their responsibility to ensure that the role of parents is seen as a positive part of the setting's community. The relationship with parents should relate clearly to the agreed descriptive statements, as they illustrate the key values and principles guiding setting practice. There should also be a parallel with the basis for the relationship between the adults in the setting, particularly between senior staff and practitioners.

If we are working to support children in their learning about social interaction and emotional understanding, we must ensure that the skill and awareness level of practitioners is nurtured to facilitate quality adult–child interactions.

The ways in which we do this will involve induction programmes and clarity of expectations, including the way in which the adults relate to each other and to the children. Developing clearly written and agreed good practice models helps to involve everyone in the process. For example, examining our routine for starting the day and the way in which individuals are welcomed can be a good starting point. Inviting those involved to say how they would like it to be provides a shared understanding and commitment to working towards improvement rather than a focus on what is going wrong at the moment.

TRAINING SESSION 2

The 'Introduction to training sessions' should be considered before delivery of each training session.

This training session relates to the text contained in Chapter 2.

Key Points

1. Five key messages.
2. Realistic expectations.
3. Language issues.
4. Partnership with parents.

Notes

The OHTs provides prompts and summaries to support developing key messages for the setting and considering ways of improving the children's experience during their time in the setting.

The aims of this training session are to:

- formulate key messages to guide day-to-day practice
- identify ways to implement the key messages
- using our knowledge of the learning process to apply to social, behavioural learning.

Activities can be selected from the following suggestions and developed to suit your particular situation. It is not essential that all activities are used but it is important that there is a balance in the delivery of the session between listening and being active.

OHT 1

- Discuss with colleagues some messages which would be appropriate to include for a setting.
- Identify who could be involved from the setting community in deciding what the five key messages will be for your particular setting.
- Working in partnership with parents is a priority theme in most guidance and good practice. List ways in which parents could be included and involved in the life of the setting. Consider how you would like to be welcomed as a new parent to your setting. By highlighting the variety of suggestions from individuals in the group, it will be possible to emphasize the importance of finding ways to ask current parents for their own views and ideas.

OHT 2

- Create an action plan or timeline which shows how a setting could work through the process of identifying and implementing their five key messages.
- Having understood that the environment of the setting makes a significant impact on the quality of each child's experience and learning opportunity, identify the following:
  - What makes us feel relaxed in our setting.
  - Suggestions of things we can do which can help children to be relaxed in our setting.

2 CONTINUED

OHT 3

- Identify what would affect your judgement about having realistic expectations about a child's response to a specific situation. For example, if a child is refusing to share a bike with another child, your judgement would be affected by the child's:
  - age
  - previous experience
  - language skills
  - level of understanding
  - usual relationship with the other child
  - previous behaviour/responses that day
  - relationship with you
  - relationship with your colleagues.

  The list can be extended in discussion with the group.

OHT 4

- Following the example which breaks down the steps involved in taking part in snack time, identify the steps involved in having lunch. Choose two of the stages and suggest ways to support a child having difficulty with these steps.

OHT 5

- Use these key points as a summary of the issues discussed in the session. Identify which elements participants feel have begun to be implemented in their setting at the present time and which they intend to focus on next.

OHT 1
Session 2

Key messages

What five things would you want to communicate about your setting?

For example:

Everyone will be welcomed to the setting

The five messages should identify principles and values which are important and agreed by everyone in the setting.

Examine each message in turn.

What would you see which would communicate the message to a visitor?

Check that each message is communicated to parents, children, staff and visitors.

For example:

All adults will smile and greet parents they encounter in the setting.

OHT 2
Session 2

Making the messages a reality

The following can be used to support and reinforce the way in which your agreed messages can be included in everyday practice:

- policies
- information to parents
- circle time
- displays around the setting
- staff meetings
- appraisal, job review discussions
- management giving positive feedback to all staff
- staff giving positive feedback to each other

OHT 3
Session 2

The learning process

Likely to include:

- watching others
- trying ourselves
- breaking down the skills
- practising each skill separately
- fitting the separate skills together
- applying the skills to a variety of situations
- improving our skill level

Supporting learning would include:

- opportunity to explore
- opportunity to use our preferred learning style (hearing, seeing, doing)
- practice
- repetition and reminder
- being given appropriate information
- opportunity to copy others
- being shown by someone who already knows
- being allowed appropriate levels of independence
- getting positive feedback about our success

OHT 4
Session 2

Snack time

In order to take part in 'snack time' a child needs to:

1. leave the previous activity
2. move to the snack table
3. find a space
4. find a chair
5. sit on the chair
6. ask for a drink
7. hold a cup
8. convey thanks
9. drink
10. put the cup down
11. stand up
12. move away from table,

as well as manage relationships with all the children and adults around.

OHT 5
Session 2

Helping young children learn

- Be clear about what the values and principles of the setting are
- Use discussion of descriptions of observable behaviour to develop a shared understanding of what everyone is trying to achieve
- Use knowledge of child development and observations to identify realistic expectations of individual children
- Review the language that children commonly use in the setting and identify the likely message being communicated
- Discuss and agree ways to create a relaxed, joyful and purposeful environment for children and adults
- Consider current routines and break them down into small steps, check expectations of children are realistic
- Ask parents their views about ways of sharing information between the setting and home
- Ask parents what information they would like about their child's day and how they would like this to be shared
- Include parents in prioritizing your five key messages about your setting

CHAPTER 3

Dealing with Conflict

In this chapter the following questions will be considered:

1 What skills do we need to communicate effectively?

2 How can we break down social interaction into skills which can be practised?

3 What can we do to help children learn how to deal with conflict appropriately?

Making connections with others is important to us. The majority of our communication is non-verbal. It is important to check out the messages we actually give and receive. We can support and plan for children's social learning including a focus on social language and the three stages of an interaction. Accepting that conflict is an inevitable part of all our lives enables us to change our negative view to one of opportunity for social learning. Adults behaviour directly affects the behaviour of the children.

Learning to Manage our own Behaviour and Finding Ways to Maximize our Communication Skills

Our lives are governed by communication and degrees of social connection. Seldom do we take the opportunity to consider what is involved in a 'successful' interaction, but we know how good it feels when it happens! Everything about us communicates something about ourselves, from the clothes we wear, the activities we choose to take part in, to the words we say.

Opportunity to reflect

If we were a visitor to our setting and met ourselves, what messages would we receive?

Consider the messages we give through our clothes, body language, verbal language, facial expressions and tone of voice.

In direct communication with each other, the key elements involved are:

- facial expressions
- body language
- tone of voice
- specific words.

Generally, research shows that 85–95 per cent of our communication is non-verbal. This should lead us to think more carefully about the way we use the other elements to get our message across. Somehow when we are communicating, particularly with children, we assume that they will not notice the difference in our tone of voice or the expression we have on our faces.

Sometimes we even think that they should do as we say no matter how we say it! The confusing result may be that adults will use a soft tone of voice or a smile when telling a child they should not do something. Children will understand that adults are talking about them, and whether this is positive or negative, well before they are skilled in their own verbal communication. Therefore, assuming that children do not understand what we say over their heads is totally unrealistic and can lead to some very unpleasant misunderstandings when children respond to what they have understood from such adult communications.

Even if children do not understand the words, they will get messages from our other communication skills. Children are very skilled at picking up meaning and intention from our body language and tone – the same words spoken in different ways will result in very different responses from the same audience. I believe that the first thing children (and adults) look for in an interaction is whether the tone and body language suggests this is going to be a pleasant or unpleasant interaction. Even as adults we make a split-second assessment before we either relax to hear and respond to what is said or we start looking for a way out or a defence. An example is the very quick response from some children of, 'It wasn't me', before you clarify what incident you are talking about. The adult defensive comment 'he's always like that, no one else can do anything with him either' before you have a chance to talk about using different strategies, is another. Both responses involve the receiver of your message feeling that the chances are you are going to criticize or blame them for something. Needless to say our previous experiences of the situation, knowledge of your usual response, guilt about something we could have done better etc. will affect how sensitive we are to reading the 'accusing' message.

The difficulty with taking this type of approach is that it has little scope for learning. The person giving the message has set the tone, the receiver is hiding behind whatever defence they can gather and there is no opportunity for joint problem-solving. The approach to a situation can often set the tone of the interaction. Being clear about the message we want to give and ensuring that our facial expression, body language and tone of voice all say the same thing, gives us the best chance of getting our message across clearly.

As adults we frequently read inaccurately communication from others. We think they are angry when they are not, we think they are indifferent we they are not etc. Children, I think, whilst frequently getting the tone right are often confused over the detail. They have, after all, had less time to practise!

This cocktail of messages and misunderstandings can only be tackled through getting to know each other more and checking out what we have understood from an interaction. Also involved in this process is checking that the message we intended is the one that got through. For example, 'I needed your help quickly because I was worried that Ahmed would get hurt' gives the opportunity for a discussion about whether this message was received or misunderstood as you being angry.

If you have had situations where communication has been confused with a particular person, it is worth reviewing ways in which you can make your message simpler and clearer. This might include choosing your time to talk, choosing a suitable place, being physically on the same level as the person you are speaking to, inviting their comments first and ensuring that your facial expression matches the message you want to give. For example, if you want to give a positive, welcoming message you would use an open, relaxed body stance, not folded arms and pointing fingers!

All this can seem very complicated but practised over time, like any other skill, it becomes easier and more effective. Helping children to learn about communication is a long slow process – after all, we as adults are still practising! There are many activities we can use to provide opportunity to practise without feeling the emotion of the interaction, which is often what causes the confusion. This can be done through the use of pictures of various facial expressions and interactions. These can be used as the starting point for discussion about what might be said, felt and thought during the conversation. Puppets, story books and prepared scenarios are further ways to help children explore with you the different ways a particular conversation could develop. Rather than trying to find a 'right' answer, it is more helpful to find a variety of different possible outcomes. This can help to follow through the choices of response to a consequence – question prompts along the lines of 'What might happen next', 'What if ...' or 'What could Sammy say to help make things feel better for Sana?'

In the real-life situation, with children in the setting, adults can help to clarify for children the message they are giving by reflecting back to them what you have understood; for example, 'You sound angry, you really want to have a turn on the bike don't you?' This can be combined with opportunities for small groups of children to suggest different words and ways of saying things to each other. Alternatively, through discussion, ask children to find phrases which could be used to ask others to play, and making a display with photographs with the phrases written in speech bubbles. This display can then be used as a reminder and prompt at the appropriate time.

Free-play situations are often thought of by adults as a lovely carefree time for children, but is often far from reality. A big space, a large group of children and a selection of equipment can be very confusing and worrying. Social language for this situation needs to be taught and children's thinking associated with the opportunities available. Preparation for going outside might include some discussion about what the children are thinking about doing first, who they might want to play with first etc.

When we think about language it is important to clarify what we really mean. The two key functions of language I would suggest are:

- to convey meaning
- to establish and hold a connection.

There are five main aspects to our experience of language, each of them complex in their own right and integral to the communication process:

- noises
- words and phrases
- associations and nuances
- body language
- facial expressions.

Changes in the noises we make, accents and different languages will affect the receiver of our message, perhaps requiring more intense listening skills or coming to terms with previous experiences of someone with a similar accent. Phrases and words may have different associations for the speaker than the listener, which will affect their shared understanding. Facial expression, body language and gesture can completely change the meaning of our words. Basically, the more you think about it the more complex the process becomes but we all manage to communicate effectively, at least with some people some of the time. It can be useful to consider that each interaction has three distinct stages.

The Three Stages of an Interaction

Every interaction has three stages, a beginning a middle and an end. We consider a child taking part in an activity with two friends.

Beginning

There has to be a way of getting into or starting the activity. Key phrases like 'Can I play?' and 'I want to play too' are likely to be used but there will also be facial expressions and body language which affect the response received to the request. Opportunities to try out different phrases and ways of saying them, and encouraging children to say if it would make them want to play or not, allows time to practise without the likelihood of it ending in conflict. Although this will not automatically change the children's behaviour and responses to each other, it will gradually build the vocabulary and range of responses that children are able to use. It is important that we look at both sides of the communication. What does it feel like to deliver the phrase and, equally, what does it feel like to be on the receiving end?

This way of working does have implications for some of our thinking about our responses to children's friendships and sharing in the setting. It is not realistic for all children and all adults in the setting to be best friends, but it is reasonable to have a consistent level of tolerance and support which is expected and encouraged. This means that the adults need to clarify and agree responses to children not wanting to play with each other or only wanting to spend time with one particular friend. The most effective approach is probably to emphasize that we have different friends related to different activities; for example, friends to build with, read with, sing with etc. It is important that we support parents to encourage this idea too, as it can be seen as a major milestone for children settling in to a new setting to have found a friend. The pressure to achieve this can be a barrier to the friendship actually happening. The other consequence is that, should the friendship end, this is seen as a disaster, not only because the friend has been lost but that the child has failed to achieve what all the adults expected. The child is left with a sense of failure which is disproportional to the actual event.

Middle

The middle part of the interaction is about maintaining connection, negotiating, finding out about each other and experimenting with ideas. We invest a lot of time and words on this section as adults. It is important to us that we give and receive messages that people want to keep talking to us, listening to us and giving us positive messages about being with us. Talking about the weather is an obvious example. It does not actually matter if it is raining or sunny but it is a common experience which we can use to make a connection with someone. Making a connection is one of the first experiences we have as very young babies and something most of us continue to seek as adults.

End

The end part of the interaction is the most likely to go wrong and the time when conflict often occurs. This is the time when we have to find an acceptable way of saying that, 'I no longer want to be here, with you, doing this activity'. The likelihood is that someone will experience feelings of rejection, disappointment or anger which will find expression in raised voices or hitting out.

There is no recipe for an immediate improvement to any inappropriate behaviour or response. However, like all learning it can be seen as a process which can be broken down into small steps or stages. For example, to help improve the end stage of the interaction described we would want to know the present frequency of conflict. From this baseline we can set our realistic expectations for improvement, if it is now ten incidents per day, initially we would be looking at a reduction to perhaps eight per day. To check progress we would want to review this after three weeks. The essential part of the process is to then decide what action the adults need to take to support the change. First, there will be some teaching required, this may be about key phrases which are acceptable ways of saying you want to leave the activity. The idea would be to begin to develop a stock of phrases from which children can select one which they feel happy to use. Inevitably, some children will already be able to make several suggestions, whilst others will need to work with one phrase for a considerable time before they are ready to experiment with others. The more subtle bit of identifying these phrases is that, while the focus is on the user of the phrase, the receiving of the phrase is put in context. If another child uses one of the key phrases to you, for example, then there is a beginning of the understanding that it does not mean that they hate you, will never play with you again etc., but just that they have had enough of this game at this moment. This begins to reduce the degree of rejection felt by some children.

There will never be a time or even a day when there is no conflict between anyone in your setting. This is the reality of life and our drive to attempt to have our own needs met in competition with the others present. Conflict is inevitable. What we need to focus on is developing a variety of ways to explore and resolve the conflict. The first step is to consider our view of conflict, trying to shift our thinking from purely negative to an opportunity for learning.

Adults have all developed different responses to conflict and it is useful to identify your own before trying to work on the children's. You may feel anxious, frightened, excited, angry or determined. Conflict and our response to it is closely related to our feelings about what level of control we find acceptable in different situations. For example, what do we think colleagues are thinking about us if the child we are working with is behaving inappropriately? If we assume they are critical of us, our response could then be to publicly blame the child so that our role and responsibility is minimized. This can lead to labelling the child as 'naughty' 'loud' or 'troublesome'. As we have already discussed, such labels lead to children making their behaviour fit the label and adults looking for proof that the label is well earned. As 'grown-ups' we have a greater range of knowledge about managing our behaviour than children. It is therefore down to us to take the initiative to change the script for the situation, children will not be in a position to do that without our help and support.

Children can experience the same range of emotions and have the same difficulty in dealing with conflict as adults. In reality the difficulty is not in the conflict but in the unresolved conflicts which we can keep returning to and adding to our belief system about conflict. For example, experience might lead us to believe that, 'I never win anything', 'If I shout loudest I will win', 'I have to win', 'Mine is the only answer', 'You're older/more senior/more confident, therefore you will win'. We can also start to look for ways of reinforcing whatever belief system we have built – 'I'm bigger than you so any conflict we have I will win' etc. This has major implications for our interactions with children because we are inevitably, bigger, more senior, older than them.

Using Conflict as a Learning Experience

(This section is based on ideas from High/Scope).

Conflict is about trying to solve a problem jointly with one or more other people. Skills we would need to achieve this would include:

- listening
- communicating clearly our own needs and wishes
- understanding
- the ability to appreciate another's view
- co-operation
- the ability to communicate respect.

If children are able to rehearse and explore the use of these skills in the emotionally safe environment which we provide for them, they will be much better equipped as they get older to deal with conflict situations for themselves. Keeping adult language short and clear is also key in helping to get the message across when emotions are running high. All that is needed is 'no hurting' rather than a long explanation that it is not nice and that we cannot let you play again if you are going to do that and what will Mummy/Daddy say, etc. If any further discussion is needed it should be left until everything is calm again and emotions have receded. None of us are able to learn effectively when our emotions are in control because our thinking is hijacked by physiological changes in the blood flow to the brain.

For the children in our setting to receive consistent messages about appropriate ways to resolve conflict it is important that the adults have had an opportunity to discuss and agree on the approach they will take. There is no magic about the process of resolving conflict, it usually covers the following steps:

1. Tell me what has happened:
    (a) take turns
    (b) listen to each other.
2. This is what I think you have said.
3. Is that right?
4. How can we sort it out?
5. What could we do differently next time?
6. What will we do now?

If we see conflict resolution as an opportunity for learning then we need to consider how the process is used to maximize learning. The way in which the adult approaches the situation and supports children to work out a solution will be a significant part of the learning.

The first step of supporting children's learning about positive conflict resolution is for the adults who will be implementing the process to agree on the process they will use and how it will be encouraged. Some key issues which can need agreement between the adults are:

- Is it appropriate for children to say sorry after an incident?
- Can more attention be given for appropriate behaviour than inappropriate behaviour in the 'sorting out' process?
- In what ways can we ensure that children receive consistent messages about their behaviour?
- Should children always share all the equipment/toys they are using?
- Do all children need to be friends all of the time?

When agreement is reached it can be useful to extend the discussion to clarify what the adults consider to be acceptable/unacceptable behaviours in the setting. Importantly, this learning should not just be focused on children who are assertive. Children who respond in a passive way need as much support to be able to use appropriate language and to deal with a conflict situation. We need to be vigilant in intervening so that passive children are not always the ones who have to give in.

In the same way that we have broken down other learning into small steps, we can approach the conflict resolution process in the same way. For example:

1. Use a story to introduce the idea of sorting out disagreements.
2. Use puppets to role-play the situation.
3. Let children suggest ways in which the characters could sort out their difficulty.

4 Use pictures and words to make a display about the first two steps of the process – talking about what happened, listening to what is said.

5 Share with all children times when the process has been successful and support children to say how things were sorted out.

Once children are familiar with the first two steps, a similar stepped approach can be used to highlight the rest of the process. As with all learning, some children will acquire the language and idea of the process very quickly whilst others will continue to need adult help for much longer. Some of us continue to need support as adults so we must be realistic and set our aim as introducing the process to young children rather than expecting them all to be able to learn to use the process independently. For very young children the first step is for adults to use the process consistently and encourage them to explore the appropriate language needed to make the process work.

The element which makes conflict resolution so difficult is the emotion we feel about the conflict itself. Therefore it can be helpful to give children opportunities to practise the process when they themselves are not part of the conflict. This can be done very effectively through role-play, stories and helping children to suggest solutions for other children. Gradually children will begin to understand that there is no 'right' answer but a variety of possible ways to sort out the problem, which can then be agreed on. This is perhaps one of the hardest stages in the process for the adults to work with as it would be so much quicker to give our solution such as 'take turns' or 'confiscating' the toy, but by doing this we reduce the learning considerably, perhaps to, 'You always win if you are bigger'.

Inclusion

There is much discussion and debate about including all children in mainstream settings. In the majority of situations adults are becoming more welcoming and willing to work with parents to include children who experience a variety of conditions and disabilities. The greatest challenge to this principle is where the child presents behaviour which is difficult to manage. This is particularly true if the behaviour includes hurting others. As professionals working with young children, our attitude to this issue has a significant impact both on the children and families with whom we work.

The reality is that all children can, and probably will, display difficult behaviour at some time and under certain circumstances, but it is the intensity and frequency of the challenge which causes adults to feel at a loss. However, generally speaking, the key with young children is to use the same basic strategies but to increase the intensity and frequency to meet that of the behaviour. Using our knowledge of the individual child we can hypothesis about what the child is communicating through their behaviour. Noting times and situations when the behaviour is most likely to occur gives the adults the opportunity to explore ways of taking action to minimize the impact of the behaviour. This basic approach is effective in both reducing inappropriate responses and gathering specific information to help other professionals focus their skills, should this be necessary.

Including social interaction in our process of breaking down tasks into small steps, using 'can do' statements, can help to identify what action the adult needs to take to best support the child. We should avoid talking for them or making decisions over their heads. Essential to this being empowering for the child, is that we ensure all adults support positive views and images of all children. Adults must be proactive in challenging 'labelling' of children as 'naughty', 'silly' or unable to do things. Rather, a positive focus on the fact that we all need help at some time with something, that we are all learning new things and that we all make mistakes is essential to a positive learning environment. In essence, all children must be treated with respect as individuals in their own right.

It is easy to develop roles with which we feel comfortable to use in group situations and to assume that we have no way of approaching a situation in a different way. Children are already doing this in our settings and, rather than following the pattern, it can be enlightening for children to be given a specific opportunity to play a different role. For example, in imaginative play situations, if a child always takes the 'leader' role an adult can help the children to change roles for the last, say, five minutes of the game. Or they can share what it might be like not to play that role next time.

To encourage children who are less confident, create situations which give them the opportunity to share particular strengths and skills. Encourage children to help each other rather than always asking for help from an adult. Where a particular activity or element of routine causes a problem children can respond positively to some advanced warning and preparation for what is about to happen. For example, 'in five minutes we need to tidy up, where will you put your model' or offering the opportunity to show the model to another adult or to have some help to put it somewhere safe etc.

Successful social, behavioural learning can be evidenced through learning stories, which explains the sequence of events and the learning which has taken place with annotated photographs providing a positive image. This can be shared as a display or kept in the story corner in book form. This gives opportunities for successful experiences to be revisited and reinforced with or without an adult.

Our aim is to help all children and adults to learn about each others' strengths in the individual's personality rather than focusing on disabilities or difficulties. Adults can often then help children to approach difficulties through use of existing strengths.

TRAINING SESSION 3

The 'Introduction to training sessions' should be considered before delivery of this training session.

This training session relates to the text contained in chapter 3

Key Points

1 Communication skills.

2 Stages of interaction.

3 Dealing with conflict.

Notes

Each OHT provides a summary and the key points from the chapter. It is not necessary to use all of the activities but it is important to vary the role of the participants throughout the session in order to support different learning styles, i.e. seeing, hearing and doing.

The aims of this training session are to:

- understand the elements involved in our communication skills
- identify ways of supporting children to learn about social communication
- use conflict resolution as a way of learning about communicating with each other.

Activities can be selected from the following suggestions and developed to suit your particular situation. The more detail identified and encouraged in discussion, the easier it will be for practitioners to put into practice. Understanding the clear parallels between adult and child learning in this session can help adults to see how difficult it is for children to manage their behaviour in the real situation.

OHT 1

- Collections of photographs from magazines. Cover up the face and only show eyebrows at first. Ask adults to guess what the rest of the face may look like. Uncover a little more at a time and continue the process.
- Try out different facial expressions and body language which together show:
  - anger
  - sadness
  - fear.

OHT 2

- Try to mix facial expressions with different body language – discuss the confusing mixture which is created. For example, smiling when saying something in an angry voice.
- Select video clips of short interactions which illustrate the influence of body language:
- Show a video clip of an interaction with no sound. How accurately can you predict the emotions being communicated?
- Say the following phrases, expressing as many different emotions as possible:
  - I want to see you.
  - Come here.

3 CONTINUED

- What have you done?
- Why are you here?
- What a surprise!
- What is your name?
- What are you doing?

■ Our own responses and feelings about activities will inevitably influence the way that we present them to the children. Consider individually and with colleagues the following:

- During which activity do you find it easiest to get involved with the children?
- If a visitor was watching you involved in this activity, what exactly would they see you doing?
- What would they see the children doing?

The more detail in which this can be described the better, because it will clarify the observable behaviour associated with the increased level of involvement.

■ Set up an activity where adults work in pairs to play a simple game, e.g. hangman. Prior to the activity give one adult the instruction that they should not under any circumstances in any way communicate with their partner. Allow signs of frustration to develop before ending the activity. Provide opportunity for sharing of feelings about the task and the roles played.

- Make a collection of phrases an adult might use to appropriately express anger or frustration.
- Suggest phrases which would be appropriate to use in an early years setting.

OHT 3

■ Language is one vehicle for communication but it gives rise to endless opportunities for misunderstanding. As adults, we accept that sometimes people say things they do not mean or attach different meanings to words and phrases. It is sometimes hard though to remember that children are just learning about the words they are using and that they have learned these words from a variety of people and situations. Within their learning experience they may not have understood the full implications or meanings of the words and phrases they use. What they probably will have picked up is the way in which the words were used and something of the response. For example, shouting 'I want it now!'gets you what you want. Therefore it is worth using the words to see if it works in another situation.

- Make a collection of phrases a child might use to express anger or frustration.
- Suggest phrases you could use to respond.
- Identify the message this gives to the child.
- Collect ideas of ways you could support further learning about responding to similar situations.
- Identify what impact the following would have on your response: a child new to the setting, a child whose first language is not English, a child who has language difficulties, a child who has difficulties understanding situations, a child aged 5 with some developmental delay.

■ In order to encourage a consistent approach to support children's social emotional learning, the adults in the setting need to make some conscious decisions. These would include:

3 CONTINUED

- Is it appropriate for children to say sorry after an incident?
- Can more attention be given for appropriate behaviour than inappropriate behaviour in the 'sorting out' process?
- In what ways can we ensure that children receive consistent messages about their behaviour?
- Should children always share all the equipment/toys they are using?
- Do all children need to be friends all of the time?

Each of these discussions will raise several points of view which need to be reconciled. The purpose is not for us to convince each other that our view is correct but to find a practical compromise which can be applied by all on a daily basis.

The situation can be depersonalized through the use of scenarios which illustrate each of the situations and allow adults to think in 'professional mode' rather than purely on a personal basis.

- As a group consider how it feels to be approached by someone who looks:
  - angry
  - frightened
  - excited
  - determined.

Collect descriptive words and record these on a flipchart.

OHT 4

- Considering the elements involved in the learning process (Chapter 2) identify a variety of opportunities in which children could learn about and practise the skills needed for conflict resolution.

OHT 5

- Plan the steps you will use to introduce a conflict resolution process to the children. Include opportunity for modelling, practice, positive feedback, review of what has been taught, reflection on how it is working with the children, how it will be shared with parents and feedback to children/parents.

OHT 1
Session 3

Communication skills

The communication skills we develop involve the use of our:

- facial expression
- tone of voice
- body language
- words

To ensure a consistent message we need to make sure that all these elements are giving the same message.

85–95 per cent of communication is non-verbal, words only count for about 10 per cent of the message.

OHT 2
Session 3

The three stages of an interaction

Beginning

- A way of getting into the interaction

Middle

- Keep the interaction going

End

- A way of ending the interaction and moving on

What phrases might commonly be used for each of these stages?

OHT 3
Session 3

How do you feel about conflict?

- Anxious
- Frightened
- Excited
- Angry
- Determined

What effect does this initial reaction have on the way you physically approach a conflict situation?

What messages would your body language, tone of voice, facial expression and words be giving?

OHT 4
Session 3

Skills for conflict resolution

- Listening
- Communicating clearly our own needs and wishes
- Understanding a situation
- Ability to appreciate another's view
- Co-operation
- Ability to communicate respect

OHT 5
Session 3

Possible conflict resolution process

1 Tell me what has happened:

(a) take turns

(b) listen to each other

2 This is what I think you have said:

(a) Is that right?

(b) How can we sort it out?

(c) What could we do differently next time?

(d) What will we do now?

CHAPTER 4

Grown-ups Make a Difference!

In this chapter the following questions will be discussed:

1 In what ways can an adult interact with a child to support their learning?

2 How can we reflect constructively to improve children's learning?

3 How can we show progress in social/behavioural learning?

The adult – child interaction is crucial to the effective learning process, therefore we need to be clear about what we need to do and what our purpose is in interacting with children. The characteristics of being open to learning include being relaxed and 'joyful' according to Maria Robinson (2003). We can use our knowledge of individual children to encourage this to happen more frequently. Learning about and managing our own behaviour will positively affect our experiences and help us to support children's learning. Children will need to interact socially as adults, and will do this most effectively if they have opportunities to learn the skills as early as possible. Professor Ferres Laevers whose research provides a method of observation developed in the Effective Early Learning Programme (Pascal, 1997), identifies the characteristics and importance of emotional well-being in the development of learning.

Getting Down to the Detail of How You Make a Difference

It would be so easy if telling someone what to do was all that was needed for them to learn something. We would no longer need schools, colleges or universities; a tape recorder or radio would suffice.

There are many ways in which we can take part in activities with children and often our choice of how we get involved will influence how much the child will learn from the experience.

We can choose from:

- playing alongside
- giving a running commentary of what the child is doing
- taking an equal part in the activity

- getting involved in joint problem-solving and discovery
- initiating reflective thinking
- extending through open-ended questioning.

The role we play, ideally, is one of a companion in a journey of joint discovery. Working towards this goal takes time and confidence, and is also more complex than it seems at first. To begin to achieve this we need to ensure that the activities we offer children are clearly planned with the learning opportunities in mind. This will inform the way adults support the learning opportunities. In these circumstances only a very small percentage of our time will need to be used for controlling behaviour and being a referee.

Children learn more from what we do and how we are day by day than what we say. They will build a picture of who we are when we are with them, in the same way that we do about them. As we have previously discussed in Chapter 2, language plays a significant part in our social learning.

All the children we work with will have different language abilities, levels of experience and be at different stages of development. Their language will be dependent on their developmental stage and previous experiences, but also on the experience we offer them. According to Maria Robinson in her book from *Birth to One* (Robinson, 2003), as human beings we are best able to learn when we are joyful: 'Joy opens our minds and hearts to new experiences, making our mental processes more creative and flexible.' The converse is also true, that mental processes are generally less efficient when people are feeling anxious.

The essence of what we are talking about is being 'in tune' with the child, being alongside them in understanding their experience of the situation, not purely interpreting from an adult point of view.

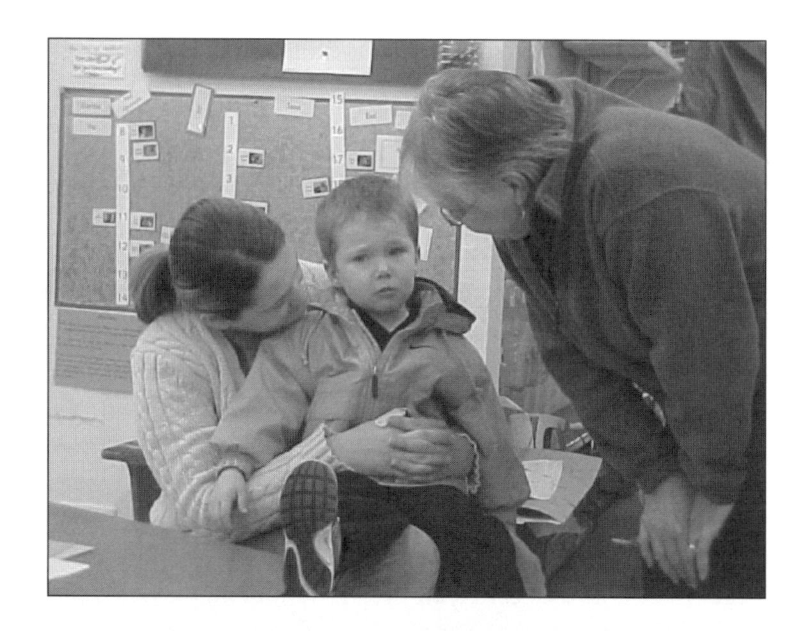

Initially, as practitioners getting to know the children we are working with, the 'quality' interaction may happen more by chance than by design. But reflecting on what sparked the child's interest, and our response, enables us to increase the number of times it happens. At first this could be just an increase of one really positive interaction each day. But from this first step, through continued reflection and sharing ideas with colleagues, we can identify the skills and approach which have the best effect. Having identified the skills, we can then make it happen more frequently. As individuals ourselves, our moods and energy levels rise and fall in the same way as do the children's. The major test of our own knowledge, understanding and management of our own behaviour is whether even on a low-energy, difficult-mood day we can still initiate a positive and joyful interaction with the children. Through striving to improve our skills in this way we develop a professional approach to our role.

Opportunity for reflection

Think about a really good interaction you experienced with a child recently.

What did you do which made it so good?

When can you try to do it again?

There are many ways in which we can manage our own behaviour more effectively. For example, reflecting on good days and identifying what was different about us and the way we did things. This may include us being less tired, happier, having more energy, being less busy, more focused or clearer about what we are trying to do. Gradually, we build up a picture of how we feel when we have the best chance of enjoying positive relationships with the children, our colleagues and, principally, ourselves. There are many things which are not in our control or are unexpected, so to give ourselves the best chance of having a good day we have to find ways of looking after ourselves within the confines of what we can control. Making conscious decisions about what we do can be one of the most satisfying activities. Realizing that there are some choices which we can make gives a sense of empowerment and control over our lives. One of the major decisions we have to make is about what work we choose to do. If we have the unsatisfying feeling of having drifted into working with children we are unlikely to enjoy or make the most of the opportunity for either ourselves or the children with whom we work. When we dread going to work it is important to consider if this is a passing feeling, or something more fundamental. If it is a passing feeling, refocusing on the positive impact you have had on the children's learning, development of relationships or ability to cope with a new routine can highlight the ways in which you are making a positive difference. If the feeling of dread is more long term and deep rooted, then identifying your existing skills gives you the opportunity to focus your search for a more appropriate working environment.

Generally, adults these days lead very busy lives and have both work and family commitments which must be met before our own needs are considered. Checking out now and again how we feel about the balance of work, looking after others and looking after ourselves in our life gives us the opportunity to reflect on possible ways to improve things. Whatever we decide will help us to give ourselves the best possible chance to cope with the stresses and strains of our lives must also be realistic and manageable. Taking more exercise may improve our energy levels, but can be hard to maintain as we get nearer to a holiday and are feeling particularly tired.

Refocusing on the positive and enjoyable aspects of our work and relationships can energize and revitalize our interest and enthusiasm. Spending time involved in an activity we enjoy, with someone we like and feel relaxed with, during which we discover something new, is a very satisfying, sometimes exciting, experience. If we take time to discover ways to give ourselves the best chance of having a positive day and combine this with planning effective learning opportunities and consistent communication skills, we can increase the likelihood of positive interactions with the children. By identifying our own communication skills using language, tone, facial expressions and body language we can begin more effectively to communicate our messages. If we ensure that all the elements of our communication are saying the same thing, we increase the chances of our message getting across. By clarifying with colleagues the messages we want to communicate and how we could communicate them, we can increase our confidence in delivery of the messages.

Social and Behavioural Learning

Children will learn about behaviour and social interaction whenever they are with us. There is nothing we can do to stop this happening. So as adults working with children we have a choice, either we leave the learning to chance and accept the consequences or we consider the key messages we want to give and find ways to communicate and teach them effectively. Our own communication with the children can contribute to our aim to be in tune and to enable children to develop their own communication skills. Partly this will be through role-modelling but also through reflection and problem-solving. For example, we can physically be at the child's level, we can listen to what they say, really listen, show we have been listening while checking our understanding through engaging in conversation and showing interest. This helps us to move away from a direct question and answer model of communication. Developing a problem-solving approach with children to explore and look for a variety of interpretations and ways of saying things can raise awareness of language and confidence in using new words and phrases. In working this way we are also able to give clear messages about how to work together, support each other and communicate with each other.

We all learn according to context, that certain language is acceptable in certain contexts and not acceptable in other contexts. For example, most children develop a home and nursery/preschool language. As adults we often use different language with children than with our adult friends. It takes a while, though, to learn the subtleties of some contexts. The response we give to children's communication and choice of words will be a key factor in making it happen to a greater or lesser extent. It will also influence the emotion the child feels and the way they react next time. Whilst there are many influences on the way we respond to children at a particular time, if we can develop a reflective professional approach we can begin to work out which response is going to be the most effective in helping the child develop their own positive communication skills.

Developing Social Language Skills

There are always social situations in which adults feel uncomfortable, but we develop ways of behaving and language which helps us to deal with these contexts. Children have had less time than us to practise these skills, and finding ways of helping them to explore possible ways of responding and awareness of how others might be feeling will be invaluable.

One of the things which can make adults and children anxious is dealing with unfamiliar situations and people. For some practitioners this anxiety may arise particularly when children with special needs are attending the setting. There are several ways in which we can begin to address these anxieties:

1 being able to talk through the anxious feelings with supportive colleagues
2 gaining information and knowledge
3 being involved in joint problem-solving
4 seeing the problem from the child's perspective
5 agreeing a way forward which is supported by the other adults involved.

As we get older we have more experiences to influence our thinking and more fears and anxieties which worry us and affect our behaviour, but not necessarily more ways of appropriately expressing our emotions. To support the children we are working with, our focus needs to be to develop awareness of the variety of positive and effective ways we can communicate our thoughts and feelings. Letting others know how we are feeling can be a risky business and their response is often unpredictable. The response adults and children receive to such risk-taking will have a specific impact on how they approach the risk again. Being able to say you are frightened among a group of friends can be a huge risk and it will only be worthwhile if the response is affirmative and supportive.

As adults we need to encourage children to develop their skills through our actions and reactions. Letting children into the secret of adult thinking, sharing times when we do not know what to do, when we find things hard, when we are happy, sad etc. can give very powerful messages about appropriate ways of communicating and sharing emotions.

Actions speak louder than words. If we are talking to children about being kind to each other but we speak to colleagues in clipped, abrupt tones we are giving mixed messages and they are likely to follow our example rather than our instructions.

Using games as an opportunity to encourage learning and practise of social language is particularly useful, as the game is the focus and sets a relaxed tone. Careful management by the adult enables significant learning to take place.

Specifically, each of the following could be the planned learning which the adult has in mind when playing a game with a child or group of children:

- asking each other to play
- turn-taking
- applying rules
- giving and receiving instructions
- negotiation
- conflict resolution

- compromise
- finding ways to decide who goes first
- what do you do when it is not your turn
- working together
- listening skills
- comparing experience
- reflecting on why a game was successful
- giving positive feedback to each other.

Our aim, essentially, is to help children develop independence in their ability to be at ease in the company of others and to be able to make significant and satisfying connections with each other. As with all other complex skills, this needs to be broken down into manageable steps. Supportive adults can then guide them through the process, at a pace which is appropriate for each individual. Our observation and assessments provide the evidence of what the child can do and identifies the next step.

This is the same learning approach which would apply to other areas of learning and a process with which we are now very familiar. In addition, the more we learn about learning and children's incredible capacity to gain skills and knowledge, the more we learn about ourselves and our impact on the children we work with.

Bringing together the skills and knowledge related to communication and social learning begins to clarify the importance of the purpose of these skills for an individual. They are not just a collection of isolated skills but tools to enable individuals to take their place in society, able to get on with those around them and have their needs met to the extent that they are able to experience a sense of well-being. My thinking about emotional well-being has been particularly influenced by Ferres Laevers (Centre for Experiential Education in Belgium). He identifies the following basic needs for each individual:

- tenderness and affection
- security and clarity
- social recognition
- to feel competent
- to have physical needs met
- to have meaning in life.

I would suggest that these elements are all communicated through interactions with others and contribute to our self-awareness. The Birth to Three Framework focuses on the competencies of young children and ways in which adults can build on this foundation. As adults, although we may not always use that particular wording, we would recognize that it is important for us to feel that we are able to be skilful and good at something. Frequently, in our work situation it is challenging to think not only about how we support children to feel competent learners, but also to identify the ways in which we encourage and appreciate the skills of our colleagues. The hardest bit is to identify that special something which tells us that the others involved in the interaction actually care about us and what we say or do.

Professor Colwyn Trevarthen, in his work with very young babies and their communication with their main carers (Trevarthen, 1993), identifies that it is the reciprocal nature of the communication which is essential. The person with whom we are communicating is in tune with our thoughts, feelings and mood, which is shown in the way that their responses connect with our communication. In the busy life of our settings it is hard to make every interaction of the highest quality, but the reality is that for those children every interaction does matter. They are learning from us about how we respond to each other and how we share feelings, experiences and learning. Children are constantly learning how to be grown-ups from the grown-ups around them.

When that interaction really works and is in tune with the child, we can bring these ideas together to give us a picture of what emotional well-being looks like. It is not a fleeting experience, but may be seen manifested intensely on occasions. It is the sense that all is well with the world and our connection with it. What we see if someone has this sense of well-being, according to Ferres Laevers, are these characteristics:

- feeling at ease
- being in contact with feelings and emotions and enjoying life
- acting spontaneously
- showing vitality and self-confidence
- open to the world and accessible
- expressing inner rest and relaxation.

These are very familiar and having identified such clear descriptions we can share this understanding with colleagues. We cannot encourage these qualities if the relationship we establish with children is based on, overdirection, fear or an emphasis on being right. The more we look for these elements the more we can identify situations and contexts which encourage and enhance the feeling. During these times children are learning to savour the feeling. Further, if we can reflect to children the emotions they are displaying and help them articulate their responses, we help them to get to know themselves.

As well as developing ideas about emotional well-being, Ferres Laevers has also led research about children's level of involvement in activities, which characterizes deep-level learning. Again he was able to identify characteristics which describe high levels of involvement in an activity:

- being mentally active
- enjoying the satisfaction of the exploratory drive
- fully experiencing sensations and meanings

- concentrating and being focused
- interested, motivated and fascinated
- operating at the very limits of their capabilities.

To encourage this level of involvement we need to provide activities and opportunities which challenge, excite and encourage children to spend time exploring and developing their understanding of the world around them. Essential to this world is the understanding of, and competency in, connecting and communicating with others.

Linked to the idea of child involvement in activities is the quality of adult engagement with the child. Within this concept Ferres Laevers identifies three specific elements:

- sensitivity – focusing on the responsiveness of the adult to the child's needs
- autonomy – the way in which the child is encouraged to experience appropriate choices and decision-making, including the respect given to those choices by the adult
- stimulation – the way in which the adult stimulates the child's interest and further engagement in the activity.

The relationship between the adult and child is crucial to giving the child the best possible opportunity to maximize their learning. It also lays the foundation for their future responses to learning situations. The Early Childhood Curriculum in New Zealand highlights that, 'Adults respond with attention and respect to toddlers' attempts to communicate their feelings of well being or discomfort' in order to develop 'a sense of personal worth and the knowledge that personal worth does not depend on today's behaviour or ability' (Ministry of Education, 1996). Providing children with an emotionally safe environment in which to make such discoveries is both an inspirational and daunting prospect.

TRAINING SESSION 4

The 'Introduction to training sessions' should be considered before delivery of each training session.

This training session relates to the text contained in Chapter 4.

Key Points:

1 The role of the adult.

2 Managing our own behaviour.

3 Using situations to highlight social and emotional learning.

4 Emotional well-being.

5 Adult engagement.

Notes

Each OHT provides a summary and review of key points from Chapter 4.

The aims of this training session are to:

- explore some roles an adult can play in children's learning
- identify ways of learning about our own behaviour and how to manage it
- understand what is meant by emotional well-being
- understand ways in which we can engage with children to support their learning.

Activities can be selected from the following suggestions and developed to suit your particular situation. It is not necessary for all activities to be completed but it is important to provide a balance between an active and passive role for participants.

OHT 1

- Discuss what is meant by each of these descriptions. Ask participants to score each one according to how easy they find relating in this way. Try to identify together why some feel easier and how skills in the harder ones could be strengthened.
- 'Joy opens our minds and hearts to new experiences making our mental processes more creative and flexible' (Maria Robinson, from Birth to One: The Year of Opportunity). Share the conditions and activities during which children appear to experience learning in this way.
- Think of a time when you felt 'in tune' with a child during an activity. What could you do to try to make this more likely to happen again.

OHT 2

- What would a 'good' day look like for you, try to identify the same level of detail as in the example.
- Think about being a child in your setting, what would a good day look like from their perspective?
- What feedback from your colleagues would tell you that you were doing a good job?
- In what way do we give the message to our colleagues that they are competent, valued and respected?

4 CONTINUED

OHT 3

- What do you do to manage your anger when you are at home, at work?
- The earlier you are aware that you are getting angry the more effective your attempts to manage your emotions are likely to be. What is your first sign that you are getting angry. Try to identify the sign before that and, over time, the one before that, etc. Each discovery will buy you a little more time.
- Which relaxation techniques are you aware of: 7/11 breathing, counting to ten, counting backwards from 20, consciously relaxing neck and shoulders, thinking of something else. Try each of them, which seems most effective for you.
- How do you manage your anxieties? Again look for first signs and a relaxation technique which works for you. Practice will make it more effective.

OHT 4

- Social language – specific activity – identify the possible social learning which could take place. What could the adult do to encourage and extend the opportunities for learning?
- Identify a variety of ways to display/share with children appropriate ways of asking to play, saying no, saying they do not want to play anymore.
- Identify ways to use ordinary activities/games and routines to model appropriate ways to ask for something, show interest in someone, respond when something goes wrong, end an activity. Select a variety of phrases which would be acceptable.

OHT 5

- Video clips: look for examples of children:

  Feeling at ease

  In contact with feelings and emotions and enjoying life

  Acting spontaneously

  Showing vitality and self-confidence

  Open to the world and accessible

  Expressing inner rest and relaxation.

- Consider the daily routine in your setting. At which times are children most likely to feel one or more of the above. What can the adults do to enhance the likelihood of the children feeling these emotions.

OHT 6

- Of the children in your keyworker group, identify activities which are most likely to result in high levels of involvement identified by the following characteristics:
  - being mentally active
  - enjoying the satisfaction of the exploratory drive
  - fully experiencing sensations and meaning
  - concentrating and being focused
  - interested, motivated and fascinated
  - operating at the very limit of their capabilities.
- What could an adult do to encourage higher levels of involvement?

OHT 1
Session 4

The adult role in children's play?

- Playing alongside
- Giving a running commentary
- Taking an equal part in the activity
- Getting involved in joint problem-solving
- Initiating reflective thinking
- Extending play through open-ended questioning

The role will change according to the particular situation but we should maintain our position as learning companion.

OHT 2
Session 4

What does a 'good' day look like for you?

It might include:

- the alarm going off as planned and getting up within ten minutes
- the children getting up after being called three times
- everyone eating breakfast
- the car starting/bus arriving on time and with empty seats
- getting the children to school on time
- getting to work on time
- receiving a smile and welcoming comment from a colleague when you arrive
- the majority of the children in your group enjoying the activities available for the majority of the time they are there
- getting positive feedback from the children about one activity that you had planned for them
- getting one positive comment from a colleague about something you have done during the day
- getting home in time to make a meal
- being able to do something **you** want to for at least thirty minutes during the evening

OHT 3
Session 4

Focusing on the positive

- Activities we enjoy
- Time with people we like
- Feeling relaxed
- Discovering new things

What helps you to feel:

- happy
- relaxed
- calm
- interested
- confident?

OHT 4
Session 4

Social learning in a game situation

Could include:

- asking each other to play
- turn-taking
- applying rules
- giving and receiving instructions
- negotiation
- conflict resolution
- compromise
- finding ways to decide who goes first
- what to do when it is not your turn
- working together
- listening skills
- comparing experience
- reflecting on why a game was successful
- giving positive feedback to each other

But would not all be focused on at the same time!

OHT 5
Session 4

Basic needs identified by Ferres Laever

- Tenderness and affection
- Security and clarity
- Social recognition
- To feel competent
- To have physical needs met
- To have meaning in life

Characteristics of well-being:

- feeling at ease
- being in contact with feelings and emotions and enjoying life
- acting spontaneously
- showing vitality and self-confidence
- open to the world and accessible
- expressing inner rest and relaxation

OHT 6
Session 4

Characteristics of involvement identified by Ferrres Laever

- Being mentally active
- Enjoying the satisfaction of the exploratory drive
- Fully experiencing sensations and meanings
- Concentrating and focused
- Interested, motivated and fascinated
- Operating at the very limits of their capabilities

Adult engagement

- Sensitivity – focusing on the responsiveness of the adult to the child's needs
- Autonomy – the way in which the child is encouraged to experience appropriate choices and decision-making, including the respect given to those choices by the adult
- Stimulation – the way in which the adult stimulates the child's interest and further engagement in the activity

CHAPTER 5

Teaching and Learning about Behaviour

In this chapter the following questions will be discussed:

1 What is involved in the learning process?

2 Why should we challenge existing routines?

3 How can we help children develop reflection, resourcefulness and resilience?

The character of our teacher–learner interaction will influence how we feel about our work. Both children and adults can be in teacher and learner roles. There are several different ways we can support children's learning. Our approach to problems will influence how we respond to the challenges the children present. Making conscious decisions jointly with other team members about how we will respond to children's behaviour helps to establish consistency. Routines need to be viewed from the child's perspective so that they do not give rise to inappropriate behaviour.

We use the Foundation Stage Curriculum and our knowledge of the children's interests to guide the creation of an exciting learning environment. This offers opportunities for individual children to find activities which maximize their level of involvement and positive experiences of learning. It is a major part of our work but not the whole story. The web which holds it all together is the quality of the relationships which are experienced.

In order to make these relationship effective and manageable we need to bring together our understanding of relationships in general and specific issues related to learner–teacher interactions. Learning and teaching occur in a variety of situations involving many different people. The teacher role can be played by any adult or any child, as can the learner role. I would argue that one of the key features which makes the learning happen is that those in the teaching role are in tune with those in the learning role. This excludes the stereotypical overdirective 'teacher' role of telling children what they should not be doing and expecting them intuitively to know what they should be doing. This approach would close down learning opportunities rather than open them up. Making that teacher–learner connection a channel for learning involves showing:

- understanding
- empathy

- support
- pleasure
- companionship.

Ideally, the relationship will be characterized by joint discovery so that, in the process of the interaction, both parties are open to learning from each other and learning together.

Learning something new is an anxious though exciting process. It is hard, in our adult role, where we revisit similar learning situations with different children, to keep in mind that for each child it is their first approach to the learning. As individuals we would have different priorities for the form of support we would like, when we approach a new and difficult task. It is likely, though, that our list would include some of the following:

- clear information about the task
- information provided in a manageable quantity
- someone who has the knowledge to complete the task
- someone to explain clearly each step to us
- a safe situation in which we can admit we do not understand
- positive feedback about our achievements
- opportunity to practise the new learning or skill
- reminders about how to apply the learning to a new situation.

As adults, the easiest way to maintain this open view of supporting children's learning is to be clear about what we see and agree with colleagues what our purpose is in spending time with children in our provision. This may not be as simple as it first seems, there are several possibilities. For example, in a school situation or in a private or voluntary setting our purpose could be:

- to look after children while their parents or carers are not available
- to entertain children and have a laugh
- to deliver the curriculum within the time available
- to learn about children and how they develop
- to teach at the pace of the majority of children in the class
- to meet up with our friends
- to provide the learning opportunities and observe the children's responses
- to earn some money.

Once you start the list it can be endless and the emphasis may change for us at different times in our lives. The reality is that if we feel that working with children is boring, frustrating and that they do not do what they should, then we need to think seriously about why we are still there and how we can change things. If we are feeling so negative it is more than likely that we are influencing the children to feel the same about being in our company. Children will follow and mirror the responses of those they see around them, particularly adults. For example, if we introduce an activity which we are enthusiastic about the majority of children will be enthusiastic too. This is especially true if we ensure that we use all our communication skills in harmony so that body language, facial expression, tone of voice and language are all giving that enthusiastic message.

Seeing the children we work with as our teachers may be our best starting point. There is, as yet, no absolute skill or method of teaching a piece of knowledge, skill or attitude. There are so many variables related to personality, previous experience, aptitude, interest and ability which will affect the learning process. Research guides us to providing an environment and opportunities which will give the best possible chance of learning taking place. However, the teacher's attitude and relationship are the elements which can make learning a reality. The idea that through our working day we will change role from learner to teacher many times will help to maintain our interest, enthusiasm and clarify our sense of purpose in spending so much time with children. Each of us is an individual. We take time to learn about ourselves in the same way that it takes time for others to learn about us. The process goes on for our whole lives. We could never say that in the short time we spend with the children in our setting that we know them completely. Therefore, there is always something else to learn about them. Our purpose in working with children is to help them to learn about what is going on around them and the ways in which they can interact with their environment. This includes learning about themselves and their relationships with other people. If we consider the amount of knowledge that an adult accumulates by the time they are 21, it would probably fill several libraries. Some of this knowledge we need and use on a daily basis, some is purely for reference, some becomes out of date and some is just developing. We never stop learning and we can continue to use our learning to change the way we respond to people and situations. Knowing that this is true does not make it easy, even though we have had 21 plus years to practise.

Children are just beginning their learning journey, and we have the opportunity and privilege of spending a little time in their lives as a guide and companion in their learning. The way in which we approach this role will not only change the children's experience but also our own, through what we allow ourselves to learn. We can set up a room full of activities and watch children play, monitoring their safety and policing their interactions. Alternatively, we can actively observe their interest and then devise and provide situations and opportunities which will enable them to explore their ideas further. Having observed the initial interest, we should consider the possible next steps and what adult support the child may need to move their thinking forward and deepen their learning. Regardless of what type of setting we are involved with or how long we spend with children this thinking can inform our approach. Our own learning is extended through observing how the child responds to the opportunity we have provided. That learning is deepened by our exploration of the most effective way of interacting to develop and enhance the experience of the children. We then have the chance to use this learning to inform the next opportunity we provide for the child.

How to Support

The quickest way to support a child in completing a task is to do it for them. The consequence is that they will not learn or gain confidence in approaching the task for themselves. The activities and experiences available to children need to be carefully considered and planned through identification of the learning which can take place. The form of support we offer must be based on our knowledge of the child and their present abilities and understanding. This is not to say that our planning will always result in an activity which matches exactly our prediction. The child will bring their own perspective to the activity and will often extend the learning in directions we could not have foreseen. This does not make our planning wrong but effective in providing the opportunity for the exploration to take place. Our observation of the exploration which actually took place then provides the new starting point for the planning of the next activity. This process seems fairly straightforward in the context of most areas of the Foundation Stage Curriculum. The document provides some guidance in the possible pathways through each area and seems logical to us as adults. It is manageable then to increase the number of steps needed for a child to build on their learning. This becomes more complex when we are thinking about social, emotional and behavioural learning. I would suggest that this is partly because, as adults, we are less confident in our understanding of our own learning in this area. I would suggest that our difficulty is also related to our struggle to identify and develop our own self-knowledge and awareness.

One of the key learning opportunities happens when things go 'wrong'. If things are always safe, if we repeat only things we know how to do, our learning is limited. It is the interface with problem-solving which gives insight into how a setting really works. As adults we have developed our own response to difficulty which probably fits one of the following responses:

- I'm so stupid!
- Get an expert.
- Make a plan.
- Why does it always happen to me?
- I can't do this!
- Fix it.
- Nothing to do with me.
- What has worked before?
- If only you hadn't … .

However, we are not always so tolerant of children showing similar responses.

Opportunity to reflect

What is your immediate response to a problem?

What might children learn from seeing you respond in this way?

In what way would you like to change this?

The more we work with particular children, the more we will learn about their responses to frustration, new learning, levels of challenge and learning style. This is the knowledge, shared and developed with colleagues, which will help us to decide the best way to support a child's learning in a particular situation. Research suggests that in order to cope and survive adversity children need to develop the skills of the three Rs:

- reflection
- resilience
- resourcefulness.

They need to be able to reflect on what has happened and identify what might be changed. They need to have the resilience to know that it is not the end of the world when something goes wrong, that things will continue and can be repaired. Finally, they need the resourcefulness to know that there are other ways of responding and to be able to generate alternative actions for next time. The young children we are working with are just beginning to have the opportunity to develop these skills. To keep our expectations in a realistic context we need to remember that many of us struggle to hold on to these ideas in some situations.

The hardest of these elements to develop is resilience but if we break it down into its component parts it seems more manageable. A recent article in *Nursery World* by Marion Dowling (2003) listed the following elements:

- having confidence and high self-esteem
- being optimistic
- being independent
- having values and beliefs
- being sociable
- being able to understand their own and other's feelings.

The most effective influence on these three Rs is the relationship with and the role of the adults. I believe that in order to create a learning environment which provides a supportive culture for positive social, emotional and behavioural learning we need to make some very conscious decisions with our colleagues. In organizing our physical environment we will think about and decide where equipment is best placed, how it is best stored, how the children will access it and how we would like it to be used.

The social, emotional and behavioural context of our room is less tangible but of equal if not greater importance. Acknowledging this leads us to try to see things from the children's perspective. Although we can never know exactly what someone else thinks or feels, we can use our experience, knowledge and skill to best guess what is happening. We can and should also involve the children themselves in creating and evolving the way the community in our room works. Many of our decisions will initially be informed by the wider expectations of the nursery or school in which we work. However, these must be employed in a thoughtful and constructive way as what seemed effective with the group of children attending five years ago is unlikely to work in the same way this year. Basic decisions about how we would like things to be in our room help to focus on the broad issues of emotional and physical safety and essential routines such as start and end time of sessions. From this foundation it is possible to develop some principles which will guide decision-making and it is likely that these will relate directly to the nursery or school aims and vision statements.

The next step is to consider what responses we will employ in specific situations which will maintain these principles for all children. This needs to be discussed and agreed with the adults in the teaching team for the room. Having agreed, for example, that hurting behaviour will not be tolerated, the adults need to think through what their response will be to a hurting incident. The more detail which can be identified at this stage the better. For example,

- including what phrases the adults might use
- realistic consequences which can be employed
- ways in which children will be supported to learn alternative ways to express frustration, anger, etc.

The ultimate challenge to this agreement is to talk through what would have an impact on our decision in specific situations, identifying, as a team, if there might be circumstances in which we would not want to use the agreed consequences or if there are situations when we would need different procedures. The decisions themselves are likely to need revision as you all learn more about the children you have in your room, but the most valuable part is the process of verbalizing, clarifying and compromising ideas. You may not be able to agree on every element, but you do need to agree on the course of action which will be employed in day-to-day practice. Agreeing principles and values does not mean that they will suddenly become a reality; the detail of the wording and the way in which they are translated into practice must be considered too. The more we can involve children in this process the better. As soon as children are able to communicate a choice, they are able to be involved in the process of deciding on behaviours and responses which will be acceptable in the situation. As previously mentioned, the way we as adults respond will say more about how the community in our setting works than any principles, values or rules. It is essential to consider our agreed responses both from the children's perspective and our own. If we have said that we will treat each other with respect, what would that look like if we are dealing with a child who has hurt someone. Note that the principle needs to apply to both the child who has hurt and the one who has been hurt. Equally, the way in which we communicate with the adults around us, parents, staff and visitors, will give the children very clear messages about how we really think we should relate to each other.

Breaking Down Tasks and Routines

Often routines in a setting are initially established for the benefit of the adults, such as the need to move children from one area to another or tidy up to use the space for another activity etc. It is helpful to review routines from the child's perspective. After all, our nurseries and schools are there to provide for the children not the adults. We are much more aware these days of the need for children to have the opportunity to complete or return to further develop an activity. Our routines can get in the way of what the children are doing rather than support their journey through the day. Deciding on the essential daily routines and keeping this to a minimum helps children to develop their capacity to deal with reasonable change but also encourages sustained levels of involvement and meaningful learning from activities. If our routines constantly involve tidying away all equipment and interrupting the flow of thinking and exploring, then they are not supporting the children to manage their own behaviour. The frustrations which arise in stopping and starting, changing thinking and being part of different relationships makes it very difficult to get involved in activities in a meaningful way.

Adults need to challenge the reasons why the children are being asked to stop an activity and tidy equipment away. This challenge should include serious consideration of alternative ways to achieve the same result; for example, using a snack bar rather than stopping all children for snack time. This allows children to elect to have their snack at an opportunity which fits with their involvement in activities. It can also increase the level of social interaction with a smaller number of children and adults during the snack time. The snack bar does not need to be open all morning and the adult can monitor if all children have had their snack. From the perspective of social, emotional and behavioural learning there is far more opportunity for adults to support children to interact appropriately with each other and with the adults present.

For some children, coming to our setting will be their first opportunity to deal with this social situation and, understandably, they will need significant help and support. Our approach needs to clarify what we are really asking for a child successfully to take part in snack time, then to identify the small step learning which needs to take place for children who are having difficulty. Finally, the adult action needed to support the child's learning can be agreed.

With experience, adults will be able to identify that there is a pattern to children's involvement in activities. The process will include the following phases:

- novelty factor, excited interest but not sure what to do
- interest, thinks there are interesting possibilities but not sure what they are
- initial success, trial and error use of material
- social interaction incidentally focused on equipment, spending time interacting with a friend but using equipment without involvement
- intended use of equipment, chooses to use equipment and exploring what it can be made to do
- sustained independent involvement in activity
- sustained involvement in activity sharing experience with at least one other (child or adult) joint learning taking place
- conscious use of equipment combined with other previously used equipment to extend play and learning opportunities
- conscious choice and use of equipment as part of a problem-solving situation which has arisen initially unrelated to specific equipment.

These different ways of using and exploring equipment will not necessarily occur in this step-by-step manner and will depend on the way in which children are 'allowed' to use the equipment. The important issue for adults is to check that the opportunities are available for all forms of involvement with the equipment. In particular, that there is sufficient time allowed for the use of the equipment to graduate from the superficial to the more involved. The level of learning will be deeper if there is more involvement in the activity.

To create an environment in which this kind of learning can take place we need to realize that children do not always find approaching or making choices about activities easy. Again, this is a process in which they may need support from an adult who is clear about the steps involved in approaching an activity and the child's existing strengths and needs in developing these skills. In the first instance, for example, a child may need a choice between two activities to make the range available more manageable. This can then be gradually increased as the child is able to make more complex choices. This is not to say that the child has to remain at the activity for the whole morning, as each time the child is ready to move on, the adult can support in the same way. Equally, some children may need a 'tour' of the activities available and the reassurance that there will be time for them to use everything at some point during the day. This can help them to relax into an activity without the unsettling feeling that they may miss something if they spend too long in one place.

As we have previously discussed, conflict and dealing with the relationships going on around the activities are an inevitable part of managing the learning environment. As managers of the learning interaction we need to check that the messages we are giving through our use of routines are consistent with our stated aims and principles. As previously described, a constructive way forward can be to agree with all staff five key messages or principles which can be consistently communicated throughout the setting. Having agreed the key messages, the most difficult task is to identify how these messages are going to be communicated in the day-to-day practice of each member of staff. Checking through how we feel we should respond to specific scenarios will help to tease out the individual views and tensions around the decision-making. There may not be a clear-cut response which will be appropriate, but the sharing of ideas and reference to agreed aims and principles will help staff to feel more confident in their approach to the situation when it arises in reality. This more confident approach will help children to feel emotionally safer and to receive a more consistent response to their behaviour.

This can be a very difficult and soul-searching process, especially for new and inexperienced members of staff. One way of tackling and depersonalizing the discussion is to consider what would be seen by visitors which would characterize the principle or message to be communicated. Through describing what would be seen by visitors to the setting which identifies the messages, all staff can begin to work towards implementing responses and action which are in line with the agreed messages.

As well as conflict, the other inevitability when working with children is change. Just when you think you have made a secure decision, something changes which makes us think we need a rethink. We can view this in two ways. Either it is a major pressure and means that it is not worth making any decisions or it is part of our own learning process and will be added to our problem-solving skills and experience base.

Relationships with people, particularly groups of people, be they big or little people, are never static but are constantly changing and evolving. From our first introduction to the group of children we are going to be working with, we try to establish a predictability and pattern to our relationship. This sense of the familiar helps us all feel safe. It does not happen quickly or easily. As a group of individuals we need to check what response we will get if we insist on a particular course of action or that our own needs are met. For example, if we throw a tantrum and cry loudly will we then be able to have the toy the other child has; if we shout crossly at a child will they never hit again? Whatever boundary we are pushing, we will have to push it several times to be certain that it will not move or to find the conditions under which it can be changed. Gradually, the more we spend time together the more the character of the group becomes apparent. We can then begin to be able to predict the responses and situations which are likely to be evident through the day. Our influence as adults on this pattern of responses is considerable. For every decision there is a behavioural consequence. If we give more attention to inappropriate behaviour, then any children in the group who seek attention will do this through displaying inappropriate behaviour. If we tend to dismiss or marginalize children's contributions or comments, they will not share with us things which are important or worrying. They will then be more likely to deal with conflict by hitting out rather than involving an adult to resolve the situation. We do need to check out now and again the response we generally see from our group of children and what messages they are giving us about the way we are responding to their needs. This may sound simplistic and, as previously mentioned, there are many other factors which are influencing the behaviour. But, children are learning to manage themselves in this group and although they may use some strategies which have worked in other situations they will not continue with them over time if they are not successful. We all behave slightly differently in each context we are in. We do not behave in the same way when at work as when we are socializing with friends, and possibly our behaviour at home is different again. We can and do continue to change our behaviour in response to those around us but this is not purely by chance. We can make conscious decisions about it and take time to amend how we react. In our group situation we can help children to gradually learn and experience success in doing this too.

It can be thought-provoking to consider that the children we work with now will be the children who look after us in our old age and the priorities we encourage them to develop may well have an impact on us again!

Inclusion

A key test of what we have discussed in this chapter is to consider just how inclusive our group and setting is in its approach to new children and adults. One of our principles may be that everyone will feel welcome and included in the life of our community. Through discussion this can be made a reality if everyone is able to share their fears and concerns about any perceived limits to this inclusion. In the same way that we talked about challenging routines, we can challenge assumptions that we would include everyone – unless they could not behave, used a wheelchair or were not toilet trained. The biggest barrier to inclusion is, inevitably, attitude, that is, the attitude of the adults, parents and children. We have already discussed at some length the way in which our responses will influence the way the children respond, but it will also affect the parents who bring their children to our setting and the other staff who work with us. If we support the inclusive principles agreed in a staff meeting but at breaktime with colleagues say that we would refuse to change a particular child or deal with their behaviour, we devalue the agreement and undermine the principle. At some time in our lives we will all feel excluded from a group or situation. The feelings we experience are not pleasant and we would not choose to put ourselves in such a situation. Equally, we have or will all experience difficulty in accessing an activity, specific learning or amenities. Whilst there is a significant difference in this being a temporary state, it is not something we would choose. We have the opportunity to use our role to advocate inclusion and to employ our group problem-solving skills to manage the practical difficulties which might arise. The major change is in challenging the 'we can't' attitude.

Parents approaching your setting to gain a place for their child do so because they have identified the positive aspects of your setting. To make one of these positive aspects your inclusive approach is to support children and adults to learn about each other in a positive and supportive way. It is essential that the key element of this approach is to get to know the individual personality and to work together to overcome barriers to participation and learning as they arise in the same way for all children. Parents will be able to identify initial difficulties which may occur and will be a fund of knowledge and information that can be used to inform the way in which barriers are overcome. It is common to consider that a child with a particular disability or condition will have the same needs and difficulties, and therefore need the same help, as every other child with that disability or condition. This is not true. We all deal with situations differently and disabilities and conditions have a range of severities. The priority must be to get to know the child and the family and, having identified the barriers together, to problem-solve each situation as it arises.

TRAINING SESSION 5

The 'Introduction to training sessions' should be considered before delivery of each training session.

This training session relates to the text contained in Chapter 5.

Key Points

1 The teaching/learning interaction.

2 The purpose of our setting and its influence on our attitude.

3 Supporting a child's learning through problem-solving.

4 Reflection, resilience and resourcefulness.

5 Patterns of involvement.

Notes

Each OHT summarizes and reviews elements from the chapter and provides opportunity for further exploration and consideration. It is not essential that all activities are completed but it is important to maintain a balance in activity levels for participants during the session.

The aims of this training session are to:

- identify characteristics of the teaching/learning interaction
- acknowledge the influence of our attitude on the experience of the children
- identify our approach to problem-solving
- explore ways of helping children to develop skills of reflection, resilience and resourcefulness.

OHT 1

- Both adults and children can be in the role of teacher or learner. Identify and share one thing which a child has taught you recently.
- As adults we have learned many skills. Which would you consider to have been the hardest to learn? Try to recall your feelings approaching the learning, being involved in it and once you had achieved it. Record similarities and differences of experience for the group.
- What support would you like if you had to learn a new skill. What would you say to ask for this help? Collect as many ways as possible to request help.

OHT 2

- If you were able to set up and run your own day nursery, pre-school or school, how would you describe its purpose? Design an advertising poster for your setting, highlighting your key purpose.
- How would you describe the purpose of your setting? Is it likely to be a combination of two or more elements? If so, arrange them in order of priority.
- What would your existing routine for tidying up look like to a child? Identify ways for adults to make the process more supportive of children's learning. Try the same process for lunchtime.

5 CONTINUED

- Set out a range of games and activities around the room. Allow the participants free choice of what they use. After three minutes stop and ask everyone to tidy up and repeat this twice. Ask for feedback, recording the comments people make on a flipchart. Reflect on what you would change in order that the experience would be more satisfying and supportive of learning.

OHT 3

- Identify your usual first response to a problem. In what circumstances would you consider it a strength? In what circumstances would you consider it a weakness?
- One of the most frequent problems we try to solve is related to children's behaviour. Try to make a list of acceptable and non-acceptable behaviours. Discuss your examples and clarify the circumstances including the age and stage of the children. Are there any situations where non-acceptable behaviours could be acceptable?
- Identify a child in your setting who has difficulty settling to an activity. Plan with a colleague a different way you can approach the situation tomorrow to make it easier for them.
- How would you respond to a group of parents who were complaining about a child who had bitten three children? Work out a script for both yourself and the parents. Try different possibilities to explore the ways in which you can change your response to improve the outcome of the discussion.

OHT 4

- Which of the three Rs, reflection, resilience or resourcefulness, would you consider to be strongest for you? Give an example from a work situation where this has helped. What thinking might help you to strengthen the other elements?

OHT 1
Session 5

The learning and teaching interaction

Characteristics

- Understanding
- Empathy
- Support
- Pleasure
- Companionship

Support we would like might include:

- clear information about the task
- information provided in manageable quantity when we need it
- someone who has the knowledge to complete the task
- someone to explain each step to us clearly
- a safe situation in which we can admit we do not understand
- positive feedback about our achievements
- opportunity to practise the new learning or skill
- reminders about how to apply the learning to a new situation

OHT 2
Session 5

Why are we here?

- To look after children while their parents or carers are not available
- To entertain children and have a laugh
- To deliver the curriculum within the time available
- To learn about children and how they develop
- To teach at the pace of the majority of children in the class
- To meet up with our friends
- To provide the learning opportunities and observe the children's responses
- To earn some money

OHT 3
Session 5

What is your first response to a problem?

- I'm so stupid!
- Get an expert.
- Make a plan.
- Why does it always happen to me?
- I can't do this!
- Fix it.
- Nothing to do with me.
- What has worked before?
- If only you hadn't ...

How do we react if a child responds in one of these ways?

OHT 4
Session 5

The three Rs

1. Reflection – ability to reflect on what has happened and identify what might be changed
2. Resilience – the resilience to know that it is not the end of the world when something has gone wrong and that things will continue
3. Resourcefulness – to know that there are other ways of responding and be able to generate alternative actions for next time

CHAPTER 6

A Framework for Developing Effective Strategies

In this chapter the following questions will be considered:

1 How can we ensure realistic expectations of children's learning?

2 How can we develop effective strategies to manage children's behaviour?

3 What can we do if the strategy does not work?

The use of a common process can help to guide our problem-solving. The use of a 'can do' statement, including a description of observable behaviour, context and time, will help to identify a realistic target. A successful target needs to include details of adult action which will support it. The purpose of setting the target is to give the child the best possible chance of success.

Any discussion about social emotional behavioural learning seems to be full of ifs, buts and maybes. I cannot decide if this is because we know too much or too little about how we each function as social human beings. We can talk about general principles and strategies but, as a practitioner, what you really want is a specific answer and suggestion of what to do tomorrow when Charlie starts banging around the room. Unfortunately, no book can do that for you but I believe that you have the skill, knowledge and ability to begin building a strategy which will start you, and Charlie, on the road to improving things for you both. It can be helpful to have a step-by-step process to work through and a framework to guide your thinking. The things we need to bring together include:

- a realistic view of what it is reasonable to expect of a child of Charlie's age, stage, ability and personality
- the desire to try to see things from his point of view to help us understand his behaviour
- a realistic sense of the time it is likely to take for things to change

- a way of managing our own responses to give Charlie the best possible chance of changing his behaviour
- the support and involvement of other adults to help us see his behaviour in the context of his learning and not as a personal vendetta against us

Finding the starting point is often the hardest but most important part of the problem-solving. The process of problem-solving is about finding a way forward; we may not get it right first time but the information we gather can all be used to keep us moving in the right direction. We cannot use statements about what we or others 'cannot do' to find a way forward. 'Cannot do' assumes that no change is possible and keeps us focused on what is going wrong. If anything, such a view would stop things improving because we start to look for evidence which proves that the child 'cannot do' something. Changing to a 'can do' gives us a positive place to start and refocuses on the fact that things have changed and can change again. 'Can do' brings us back into the realm of learning and developing, which we can all believe in because working with children daily we see them gaining new knowledge and skills all the time.

As a form of baseline information, 'can do' statements can be a very effective means of identifying not only where the child's learning is at this point in time, but also the realistic next steps to be tackled. We are used to making observations based on children's responses to learning situations and to draw conclusions about the next steps in their learning. We do this by identifying what the children show us they can do and, through our knowledge of child development, the appropriate curriculum and the learning process, we provide learning opportunities for the next step of learning. This same process can be applied to social, emotional and behavioural learning. It feels harder for us, as adults, because the next step is not always so clear or our emotions get in the way of seeing the detail of what the child can do. Using a formula to construct a specific 'can do' statement helps to remove some of the emotion and to sort out the wood from the trees. First, however, it is useful to look at what we are asking of the child. By noting each detailed step a child needs to achieve to accomplish the whole task, we can get some sense of whether our expectations are realistic. This will then inform our observation and help us to identify where exactly in the process the child is experiencing difficulty. The elements which identify clearly and specifically what the child can do are:

- a description of the observable behaviour
- the context in which it happens
- an indication of the duration or time involved.

If we include the three elements of time, context and observable behaviour, we are able to make a statement which is easily shared with other adults and, if appropriate, with the child: for example, Zubin can sit still and quiet at storytime for two minutes. Initially, it is helpful to build a bank of 'can do' statements which are focused around the situation which is highlighting the difficulty.

For example, to take part in group storytime a child would need to:

- leave the previous activity
- tidy up the equipment
- put the equipment away
- move to the story area
- find a place to sit on the carpet
- sit in the available space
- sit in close proximity to other children
- respond to adult instructions
- look at pictures in the book
- listen to words in the story
- show an understanding of the words in the story
- respond to elements of the story
- respond to adult questions related to the story
- accept the end of the story
- move away from the story area in response to adult direction.

If we then carry out a short observation of Charlie joining and taking part in storytime, we can gather specific information which will show which of the steps in the process he is able to manage at the moment. From our observation we can then draw out the specific 'can do' statements for Charlie.

For example, we may have something like the following list of statements:

Charlie can:

- finish an activity, within two minutes of an adult request to end the activity
- put equipment into appropriate container with adult help within three minutes of the request

- walk to the story area avoiding obstacles by the straightest route within two minutes of adult request
- find a place on the carpet within one minute of adult request
- sit on carpet with adult support within three minutes of group instruction
- sit next to other children with adult support for one minute
- respond to adult instruction to be still for ten seconds
- look at pictures in a story book for the whole story
- retell some parts of a story immediately after hearing it
- show sadness and anger appropriately in response to a story
- identify up to three characters in a story immediately after hearing it
- acknowledge the end of a story and choose the next activity within two minutes of being asked
- locate an activity and begin using equipment within five minutes of having made his choice.

From this bank of statements we can then prioritize the things we feel need to be our focus. From the example, it is likely that you would decide to work on supporting Charlie to increase his ability to sit on the carpet with the other children for longer. So the particular 'can do' statement we will focus on will be: 'Charlie can sit next to other children at storytime with adult support for one minute.'

There are other 'can do' statements which will need attention over time, but trying to work on them all at once would make it harder for Charlie to progress and would dilute the effect of our strategy. Also at this stage in the process it is acceptable for Charlie to need adult support to find the most appropriate place to sit. It is also likely that the ten seconds for which he can presently manage to sit still, in response to adult instruction, will increase if he is more relaxed and we focus support correctly.

Our statement can easily be developed into a target by changing one element. Either we want to see the same observable behaviour in another context or for longer in the same context. To follow through our example with Charlie we will set the target as: 'Charlie will sit next to other children at storytime with adult support for three minutes.'

Although other children may be able to manage ten or even 15 minutes, it would be too much to expect Charlie to be able to make such a huge step in managing his behaviour, even with support. That is not to say that we can only read three-minute stories to Charlie, but we do now have to decide on what the adults will do to help Charlie to achieve his target.

This should be based on finding ways to prepare for, practise, prompt and praise the appropriate behaviour, for example, as follows.

Prepare

To help a child have the best possible chance of success it is important that we help them to prepare for the activity. This may include a reminder of previous success, but should not include a threat of 'if you don't do it as well as yesterday' etc. It is more supportive to identify things which helped the success last time such as 'I remember you put your hands on your knees last time' etc. Each attempt is a new start, and just because Charlie has improved on one occasion does not mean he will suddenly be able to do this every time. It is the adult role to identify anything which is contributing to make it difficult for him and to try to enable him to overcome the difficulties. Other preparation might include sharing a photograph of previous success and thinking about where it would be best to sit, including consideration of reaction to other children. Again this must be done in a positive context with phrasing such as 'you found it easier sitting with Ahmed last time' rather than 'don't sit next to ... '.

Practise

It is likely that Charlie sees himself as the child who cannot sit still at storytime and who is being reminded of this frequently by the adults and children around him. To help him change this view it can help to have some time with a very small group, or individually with an adult, to practise sitting still and calmly for perhaps one minute. The best way to do this is in a game context, particularly considering that we learn best in a relaxed and 'joyful' frame of mind. Once the minute is up it is really important to reflect back to the child that they have succeeded and to suggest what might have helped them to manage, for example, the way they positioned their legs, where they placed their hands or what they were thinking about. Usually children are expected to find these things out by trial and error but some of us take much longer to learn in this way than others.

Prompt

Various prompts can be used to help maintain the desired behaviour and to give positive attention and feedback. It is important that these do not disturb the story or distract other children. Simple gestures such as a 'thumbs up', a smile or a wink can signal approval and can be used for other children who also need a little help. Such signals can also be delivered by the storyteller and do not necessarily need another adult.

Praise

We all respond differently to praise and prefer expressions of approval to be delivered in different ways. For some of us, public verbal praise is just too much and we may respond by behaving inappropriately to change the attention to a form we are more used to receiving. It takes time to check which works best with which children, but starting with less public acknowledgement is a good way to begin. Praise can also be used to encourage other children to modify their behaviour, particularly in a group situation. This can be done by delivering specific praise to the nearest child who is demonstrating the behaviour you wish to encourage. For example, Charlie is struggling to maintain his sitting still but Joel is managing to remain still and quiet. Rather than commenting that Charlie is not sitting still, make no comment to him. Instead say to Joel, 'You are sitting still and quiet Joel, well done'. This gives Charlie the message of what he needs to do to get the same attention and it is likely that he will make a change to his behaviour. You then need to follow this quickly with the same level of specific praise to Charlie. As in all adult communication with children our message will be clearer if all our communication skills, facial expression, body language, tone and words/signals are working in harmony.

As you will have shared your initial concerns with Charlie's parents about needing to support him during storytime, it is essential that your 'can do' statements and targets involve parents' views and ideas of ways to support Charlie.

Opportunity for reflection

What elements would make a really good interaction with a child?

What would you include in a bank of 'can do' statements for yourself and the interactions you have with the children in your group?

Problem-Solving

Sometimes the difficulty in getting to a workable 'can do' statement and target is that our thinking is hijacked by the emotion of the situation. We are so close to the situation on a daily basis we are unable to see anything other than a 'problem'. At this point it is essential to discuss the 'can do' statements and the proposed targets with a colleague who is not so closely involved with the situation. If we are not careful the focus becomes the child as a problem rather than the opportunity for new learning. Working with a colleague through the process and framework described, gives us the chance to think about it in the same way as any other area of learning, it also gives us some shared experience to return to if we need to adapt our target. It is important to remember that it is never that a strategy has not worked just that we did not get the response we were expecting. However, whatever response we did get will tell us something more about the child, the situation or ourselves. This information should enable us to refocus the target and possibly add to the 'can do' statements and adult actions.

This involvement of the emotions is true for the children as well and, if the target we are working on has some relation to conflict resolution or interaction with others, it is important that the time and opportunity to practise is set up in a way that minimizes the emotional element. For example, if we are working on turn-taking there may be certain children or activities which, whilst still interesting, do not set the child up for levels of excitement which overtake his attempts to wait for his turn. The guiding principle is that we are trying to facilitate the child's successful learning not setting up hurdles or obstacles to prevent progress.

Often one of the most difficult things to deal with, particularly when trying to change inappropriate behaviour, is the sense of helplessness and frustration about what we as adults can do to influence the change. If we focus our attention on the learning which is needed, and apply our knowledge about how we usually help learning to take place, we have more chance of being effective. This does not mean it is an easy process but at least we are clear about what we are going to do, why we are doing it and what we hope will happen as a result. The sharing of this problem-solving approach with parents and colleagues helps considerably in the refining of the detail and begins to increase the chance of consistency of response to the behaviour and the child. The ideal is that adults at home are included in the process and are encouraged to find ways of supporting the targets at home. This can mean that a reward system of some kind is used at home to give the child the clear message that adults at home and adults in the setting are working together. It is not necessary for this reward to be either financial or tangible; often the most effective is guaranteed time with an adult involved in a specific activity. The important bit is that the reward is appropriate to the child's age and stage, and delivered as promised. It would not be appropriate for example to agree that a 2-year-old would receive a ten-minute story session with Dad at the end of the day for turn-taking on the bikes first thing in the morning. This is too far away from the event and the child will be unable to connect the two situations.

As practitioners, we often find it difficult to identify the appropriate reward for a particular target and it is likely that parents will feel at a loss when first involved in the process. It is part of our role to work in partnership with parents, so combining our knowledge and experience of child development with an understanding of the individual child. In order for this to work there needs to be considerable discussion to gain a shared understanding of the child and the way he responds both at home and in the setting. It can feel that initially you are talking about two completely different children. As we have said previously, our behaviour is different depending on where we are and who we are with, and obviously this is the same for children. In fact, for most of us, children are dealing with two significant changes in their lives while they are with us. First, they are learning to cope with the social expectations of being part of a group. Secondly, they are developing their independence and coping without their significant carers. This is a bit of a steep learning curve to say the least.

It is all very well to work at this level of detail for one child but many of us deal with up to 30 children at a time. For us to be able to manage the balance between individual and group needs, the individual targets should be part of a bigger picture which supports all children's social, emotional and behavioural learning.

Having examined the detail of developing and implementing a target for an individual child, we can use the same process to consider how such an approach can be employed when there are more children in the group, each with their own needs. Learning about behaviour and social interaction is a process and, in common with other areas of learning, children will progress at different rates. If we bring together the elements of the process already outlined, we can apply it to a larger group of children.

The easiest way to begin is to think of an empty room with no children and no adults. We have already agreed the principles and values for the setting generally, so this will be our starting point. From these key messages we can begin to think about how we would like it to be in our room. What exactly do we want it to look like? If there was a conflict between children what would be said and done to sort it out? Once you have devised a plan of how a variety of scenarios would be worked through, it is worth checking if the responses are still in line with the original key messages.

The next step is to begin to identify what learning will need to take place for the children to begin to be able to respond appropriately in the group situation. This forms the priorities for our social, emotional and behavioural curriculum for our group. Most of our priorities will be represented in relevant documents such as the Foundation Stage Curriculum and the Birth to Three framework which can help identify the specific teaching which needs to take place. Other resources such as magazines, journals and books are useful at this stage to provide ideas and suggestions for activities and approaches which you can use. Involving parents at this stage can also be very supportive, before there is a specific problem, and explains what you are doing to be proactive in helping all the children to learn about appropriate responses. You also then have more chance of parents being able to support what you are trying to do.

The timescale of the learning will be similar to the other areas of the curriculum so it is important to amend our expectations accordingly. It would not be realistic for example, to expect that having used one activity and one story session to focus on a particular element, that the children will have learned and be able to apply their learning to a real situation. As with all learning, some children will pick up the idea very quickly and almost seem to have known it already. Others will take time to work out what they are expected to do and to find a way of overcoming their usual response in favour of what you want them to do. Generally speaking, the majority of the group will respond to your initial teaching and positive attention from the adults. The rest will need some further activities and opportunities to practise your suggestions. Finally, there will be a small number of children who will need individual targets and support to be able to change their behaviour.

No matter which group the children are in, they will all need frequent reminders and positive attention for their appropriate responses. There is a tendency once we experience some initial success to stop giving the positive responses and expect children to continue with their new behaviour on their own. But relative to the length of time they have been using their previous response it is still very new learning and they will continue to need our support and encouragement to maintain the appropriate response.

To recap, the steps in the process would be:

1 Discuss and agree with the adults involved the key messages which describe the values and principles which we want to guide our practice.

2 Clarify what it will look like if the values and principles are having an effective impact on our day-to-day practice by discussing specific scenarios and agreeing responses.

3 Consider and plan the ways in which all children will be supported to learn about the responses and behaviours which are appropriate to being in the group.

Putting this process into practice is about prioritizing the social, behavioural learning which is necessary for children to be able to manage their relationships within the group. For example, finding appropriate ways to resolve conflict, learn about turn-taking, sharing and social language. As with all new learning, the majority of children will be able to access it after the initial teaching and opportunity to practise, but it is important to plan to review and refocus on the responses at regular intervals during the time the children are with you.

I have had comments from practitioners that they agree that their positive approach does improve the children's behaviour but that it is too much effort for them to keep up the positive approach. No one is expecting us to be perfect, but there are two key points to consider:

1. We have a responsibility to the children we are working with to do our best to help them.
2. Employing a positive approach in the long term will make the process more satisfying and effective for ourselves.

If we can aim for a ratio of five positive comments to one negative comment, we will have a significant impact on the atmosphere of the room. Focusing the attention that we give to positive behaviours will encourage children to try to gain our attention through appropriate responses rather than inappropriate ones.

Further criticism of this approach to children's learning about social, emotional and behavioural issues, focuses on the fact that it takes too long and too much time to change children's behaviour. I find this quite hard to accept. I can identify with the feeling of frustration and the need to deal with our own new learning of a different approach. However, adults seem happy to spend significant amounts of time talking to a child about what they should not do and the way in which they should not do it. I do not think, from my experience, that any greater time is involved in using the positive approach, although it may be more intensely focused initially. I have yet to find a situation where using this negative approach changes a child's behaviour in the long term and has associated deep-level learning. It is more likely that the inappropriate response will be redirected into another inappropriate response or the focus is changed to 'not being caught'.

All children will need ongoing support to use the suggested responses, but the majority will be able to begin to explore the use of the new learning and they are then able to role model implementing the responses. Reviewing and offering further teaching and practice opportunities will enable a further group to be able to use the ideas but it will also reinforce the message for those who have assimilated the learning. Finally, it is likely that a minority will continue to need individual targets and additional teaching to support their learning for most of their time involved with education. This may sound dispiriting but, in reality, as adults we are still regularly struggling with the need to manage our own behaviour in a variety of situations. Sometimes this is easier if we are able to wear our 'professional mask' and to fit our behaviour to our view of ourselves as practitioners working with children. Our aim should be to try to use our own powers of reflection, resourcefulness and resilience to learn about our own behavioural responses and develop a secure sense of emotional well-being.

TRAINING SESSION 6

The 'Introduction to training sessions' should be considered before delivery of each training session.

This training session relates to the text contained in Chapter 6

Key Points

1. Developing a practical approach to social, emotional and behavioural learning.
2. Constructing a useful 'can do' statement.
3. Making the statement into a supportive target.
4. Making social, emotional and behavioural learning part of our practice.

OHT 1

- Think of a child you are working with at the moment. Consider each of these elements and how you will approach them:
  - a description of the observable behaviour
  - the context in which it happens
  - an indication of the duration or time involved.

  Share with a colleague which will be the easiest.

OHT 2

- Using a video clip (or sample observation notes) of a child involved in activities, collect a bank of 'can do' statements. The video clip can be shown more than once and it needs to be acknowledged that the time element will be easier to record in the real situation.

OHT 3

- Identify the priorities for further action. Use the 'can do' statement to set an appropriate small step target.
- Identify the adult action – prepare, practise, prompt, praise.
- Set an appropriate review date. Identify the possible outcomes of the review.
- Outline the discussion the keyworker will have with parents/carers – identify key phrases which could be helpful to communicate your level of concern and the context of the child's progress.

OHT 4

- Identify your five key messages which you would like to communicate to everyone in your setting. Describe how you would maintain the key messages in the following situations:
  - conflict between two children
  - a colleague disagrees with your decision to let a child play outside
  - a child completes a task surprisingly skilfully.

OHT 1
Session 6

Problem-solving framework

We need to bring together:

- a realistic view of what it is reasonable to expect of a child of Charlie's age, stage, ability and personality
- the desire to try to see things from his point of view to help us understand the behaviour
- a realistic sense of the time it is likely to take for things to change
- a way of managing our own responses to give Charlie the best possible chance of changing his behaviour
- the support and involvement of other adults to help us see his behaviour in the context of his learning and not as a personal vendetta against us

OHT 2
Session 6

Constructing a useful 'can do' statement

Each statement needs to include:

- a description of the observable behaviour
- the context in which it happens
- an indication of the duration or time involved

Collecting a bank of 'can do' statements can help to be more specific about the difficulty the child is experiencing. For example, Charlie can:

- finish an activity in response to an adult request within four minutes
- put equipment into appropriate container with adult help within three minutes
- walk to the story area avoiding obstacles by the straightest route within two minutes
- find a place on the carpet within one minute
- sit on the carpet with adult support within three minutes
- sit next to other children with adult support for one minute
- respond to adult instruction to be still for ten seconds
- look at pictures in a story book for the whole story

OHT 3
Session 6

Prioritizing what we need to do

From the example of Charlie it is likely that you would decide to try to help him to sit on the carpet for longer with the other children.

The present 'can do' statement is:

Charlie can sit next to other children at storytime with adult support for one minute.

The target would then become:

Charlie will sit next to other children at storytime with adult support for three minutes.

The adults will support Charlie to achieve his target through helping him:

- to prepare
- to practise
- by prompting
- by praising

OHT 4
Session 6

Making social and emotional learning part of our everyday practice

The process would involve:

1 Discussing and agreeing with the adults involved the key messages which describe the values and principles which we want to guide our practice

2 Clarifying what it will look like if the values and principles are effectively impacting on our day-to-day practice by discussing specific scenarios and agreeing responses

3 Considering and planning the ways in which all children will be supported to learn about the responses and behaviours which are appropriate to being in the group

Final OHT
All sessions

Reflective thinking

Think about and complete the following:

I have learned these things about myself:

I have learned these things about children:

I will make these changes to my day to day practice:

I have made these decisions about my job:

REFERENCES

DfES/QCA (2000) *Curriculum Guidance for the Foundation Stage*. London: QCA.
DfES (2001) *Ofsted National Standards*. London: Ofsted.
DfES (2001) *Special Educational Needs Code of Practice*. London: DfES.
DfES (2003) *Every Child Matters*. London: DfES.
DfES (2004) *Removing Barriers to Achievement: The Government's Strategy for SEN*. London: DfES.
Disability Rights Commission (2002) *Code of Practice for Schools Disability Discrimination Act 1995*. London: The Stationery Office.
Dowling, M. (2003) 'All about resilience' *Nursery World*, 6 November.
High/Scope (1998) *Supporting Children in Resolving Conflicts* (video).
Laevers, F. (2000) 'Forward to basics! Deep-level learning and the experiential approach,' *Early Years*, 20(2), pp. 20–29.
Ministry of Education (1996) *Te Whariki*. Wellington, New Zealand. Early Childhood Curriculum Learning Media Ltd.
Pascal, C. (1997) 'The Effective Early Learning Project and the National Curriculum', in T. Cox (ed.), *The National Curriculum and the Early Years: Challenges and Opportunities*. London: Falmer Press.
Robinson, M. (2003) *From Birth to One: The Year of Opportunity*. Buckingham: Open University Press.
Sure Start (2002) *Birth to Three Matters: A Framework to Support Children in their Earliest Years*. London: DfES.
Trevarthen, C. (1993) 'The function of emotions in early infant communication and development', in J. Nadel and L. Camaioni (eds), *New Perspectives in Early Communicative Development*. London: Routledge.

SUGGESTED FURTHER READING

Bruce, T. (2001) *Learning through Play: Babies, Toddlers and the Foundation Years*. London: Hodder & Stoughton.

Cole, J. et al. (2001) *Helping Young Children Learn through Activities in the Early Years*. London: Hodder & Stoughton.

Cowan, D. et al. (1992) *Teaching the Skills of Conflict Resolution*. Smallwood.

Dowling, M. (2000) *Young Children's Personal, Social and Emotional Development*. London: Paul Chapman Publishing.

Elfer, P. (1996) 'Building intimacy in relationships with young children in nurseries', *Early Years*, 16(2), pp. 30–34.

Evans, B. (2002) *You Can't Come to my Birthday Party! Conflict Resolution with Young Children*. New York: High/Scope Press.

Greenfield, S. (1997) *The Human Brain*. London: Weidenfeld & Nicolson.

High/Scope (2003) *It's mine! Responding to Problems and Conflicts* (video).

Lindon, J. (1999) *Too Safe for their Own Good? Helping Children to Learn about Risk and Lifeskills*. London: NEYN.

Lindon, J. (2001) *Understanding Children's Play*. Cheltenham: Nelson Thornes.

Roberts, R. (2002) *Self-Esteem and Early Learning*. London: Paul Chapman Publishing.

Robinson, M. (2003) *From Birth to One: The Year of Opportunity*. Buckingham: Open University Press.

Whalley, M. (2000) *Involving Parents in their Children's Learning*. London: Paul Chapman Publishing.

INDEX